Anthony Miller's *Treasures New and Old* offers a stimulating account of several key characters and contributions to a significant strand of the Anglican tradition.

– Rev Dr Ed Loane, Warden, St Paul's College, University of Sydney

Treasures New and Old is a fascinating and very accessible study of the distinctive character of the Anglican way of being a Christian. At a time when Anglican identity is being contested yet again, Anthony Miller provides an historic overview of key figures and doctrines that have formed our particular spirituality, both for individuals and for the ecclesial community. Anyone searching for an historic, orthodox, authentically human, generous, inclusive and thus a liveable faith, will find much to encourage them on the way as they are accompanied by the hearts and minds we have been gifted as Anglicans.

– Rev Canon Dr Colleen O'Reilly, AM, former Chaplain, Trinity College, Melbourne

In *Treasures New and Old* Anthony Miller brilliantly captures the colourful history and rich liturgical heritage of the Anglican tradition. By reflecting on masterworks such as the *Book of Common Prayer* and the King James Version of the Bible, as well as exploring the life and work of some of its significant theologians and liturgical movements, the often tumultuous history of Anglicanism is skilfully brought to life.

– Rev Dr Daniel Dries, Rector, Christ Church St Laurence, Sydney

TREASURES NEW & OLD

THREE CENTURIES
OF ANGLICAN THOUGHT
& SPIRITUALITY

ANTHONY MILLER

Published in 2022 by Connor Court Publishing Pty Ltd

Copyright © Anthony Miller

All rights reserved. Not to be reproduced without the permission of the Copyright holder

Connor Court Publishing Pty Ltd.
PO Box 7257
Redland Bay QLD 4165
sales@connorcourt.com
www.connorcourt.com

ISBN: 9781922449993

Cover Design by Ian James

Cover illustration: Coventry Cathedral, Warwickshire. At left, St Michael's Church (14th-15th centuries), which became a cathedral in 1918 and was bombed in 1940. At right, the present St Michael's Cathedral (1956-62).

Photograph by DeFacto, licence Creative Commons Attribution-Share Alike 4.0 international license.

Printed in Australia.

CONTENTS

Foreword
Rev Professor Brian Douglas   vii

Introduction: The Anglican Contribution   1

1 The Book of Common Prayer   9

2 The King James Bible   21

3 John Jewel   31

4 Richard Hooker   41

5 George Herbert   57

6 Jeremy Taylor   77

7 William Law   93

8 John Keble   111

9 Tracts for the Times: Theology of the Church   123

10 Tracts for the Times: The Catholic Nature of the Anglican Church   139

11 Tracts for the Times: Spiritual Life, or the Doctrines in Practice   155

Illustration Credits   165

Index   167

Foreword

Reverend Professor Brian Douglas
Australian Centre for Christianity and Culture
Charles Sturt University, Canberra

Rowan Williams, during the time he was Archbishop of Canterbury, wrote a short book, *Why Study the Past? The Quest for the Historical Church*.[1] Williams's book has valuable lessons for today's church. First, he argues that history is a set of stories told to help us to understand who we are and the world in which we live.

Second, he believes that we study the past in order to see the divine at work in the lives of others, and the ways in which this work derives from God. Third, we study the past so that both traditionalists and progressives can be surprised by it, even if traditionalists sometimes do not question it, and so that progressives do not miss the point because they do not expect the past has anything to offer our modern world.

Anthony Miller's book, *Treasures New and Old: Anglican Thought and Spirituality*, shares Williams's aims. Miller tells the stories of the past so that the treasures and the wisdom of Anglican thought and spirituality can help us to know ourselves and the world in which we live. He also allows us to see the divine as present in the work of Anglican writers, the Scriptures, and liturgies. Miller helps us to see that we can come to know the presence of God through the experience and wisdom of others.

Treasures New and Old spans the ages from the sixteenth to the nineteenth century, gathering together a feast of writing, thinking, and spirituality which at times surprises us and helps us to know the old in the presence of the new. This is an admirable aim, and Miller achieves it with a very readable and incisive treatment of people, books, and ideas.

Enlightenment thinking has brought our world and our lives many wonderful benefits through scientific and empirical methods. We are richer in our lives because of these benefits, but at the same time it can be argued that since the time of the Enlightenment there has been what Professor David Brown calls "a disenchantment of the world."[2] In this process, things of this world are no longer seen as the means of God's abundant grace. A propositionalism overtook the sense of enchantment and a word ontology assumed a priority at the expense of a sacramental or even poetic view of the world.

In more recent times there has been a re-enchantment of the world to some extent, and people have come to value mystery and the supernatural as a way of seeing the presence of God. This has certainly been the case in the Catholic tradition of Anglicanism where the Eucharist has become the central act of Sunday worship, embraced by all the people of God as a work of liturgy done together. It is there that the divine presence is known and works powerfully in people's lives and faith. It is this enchantment that Miller grasps as he examines the thinking of Anglican theologians, writers and thinkers.

Richard Hooker and George Herbert, for example, two writers who figure prominently in this book, explore what in modern times has been called "a sacramental poetic."[3] For Hooker and Herbert, the language of a sacramental poetic is concerned with both divinity and the creatureliness of material things, and the way the creature or material thing, such as water in baptism or bread and wine in the Eucharist, but more broadly any material thing, can instantiate, that is, be an instance of the divine through sacramental means. At the same time, they acknowledge that the creature or material thing is not divine, even if the divine chooses to use the creature as a vehicle of grace as a sacramental poetic in a realist analysis.

Sacramental poetics points beyond itself to reveal the enchantment of the divine. Miller's skilful use of both of these writers (and of others like Jeremy Taylor) allows us to see that enchantment, to know the stories of the past, pointing us to the divine, and to see that they might surprise us. The value of Miller's book is that it helps us not to miss the point of the poetic – the reaching beyond the words to the divine. This process applies as much to prose as it does to poetry, and Miller enables us to see its implications in this in relation to sacramental theology. Some may well be surprised by the realist language used by the Anglican reformers in relation to the Eucharist, but here is the power of Miller's book.

The beauty of the Book of Common Prayer and the King James Version of the Bible contains riches of spirituality which reveal the divine among us, and Miller brings this richness, or these treasures, out to effect. These stories of the past, made new in their reading and use, show us God and help us to know who we are in the world in which we live today.

The Book of Common Prayer, for example, occupies an important constitutional place in the life of many Anglican Provinces, not least in the Constitution of the Anglican Church of Australia where it remains "the standard of doctrine and worship" and so the yardstick by which we frame and judge our belief and liturgy. It is good therefore to have a clear exposition of the Book of Common Prayer and its history so that this story can be clearly told in the modern age and the workings of the divine seen more clearly. More than this, and perhaps more importantly, Miller points to the enchantment we find in the Book of Common Prayer. Take, for example, his treatment of the Collect for St John the Evangelist where he highlights the "verbal dazzle" created by the word "light." Here is the poetic, pointing beyond itself to the very presence of the light of God. Miller's work encourages us to go back to these treasures, experience them again and, in so doing, not only to hear the stories of the past but to come to see the divine, beyond the words, as a sacred poetic.

Other aspects of Miller's book embrace more controversial aspects of the Anglican historical and spiritual tradition. He helps us to understand, for example, the Tracts for the Times (a set of tracts written by the members of the Oxford Movement) as they came to embrace the Catholic tradition of Anglicanism, which they argued had always been there. The way that the tracts treat the Thirty-Nine

Articles, for example, in Newman's Tract 90, would be for some Anglicans a challenging experience, since they could be forced to evaluate their own position in the context of difference. It is healthy for us all to do this, and perhaps there will be some things that will surprise us or that we had previously missed in our own tradition. Herein lies the essence of Miller's achievement.

Miller's work is scholarly but not burdened by tortuous argument. His method is to display the story of the writing and the person and, in so doing, to let the poetry of the words speak the story, surprising us and showing the presence of the divine, as a pointing beyond to a greater light and power. This is the real worth of what has been done. Miller, in helping us to see the treasures new and old, not only tells the stories. He also points beyond the words themselves to the divine, and this can surprise and startle us.

Anglicans of all traditions will benefit from reading this book. It is sufficiently "catholic" (in the true sense of this word, as Miller rightly observes in his essay on John Jewel) to show us the wisdom of others and to reveal the treasure new and old.

* * *

The Reverend Professor Brian Douglas is Research Professor, Australian Centre for Christianity and Culture, Charles Sturt University, Canberra, and Editor, *Journal of Anglican Studies*, a Cambridge University Press journal.

Endnotes

[1] London: Darton, Longman and Todd, 2005.

[2] *God and Enchantment of Place: reclaiming human experience* (Oxford: Oxford University Press, 2004).

[3] See Regina M. Schwartz, *Sacramental Poetics at the Dawn of Secularism: when God left the world* (Stanford, Calif.: Stanford University Press, 2008).

Introduction: The Anglican Contribution

"Every scribe which is instructed unto the kingdom of heaven is like unto a man that is an householder, which bringeth forth out of his treasure things new and old" (Matthew 13:52). The scribes who are introduced in this book are some of the great writers of Anglicanism, who study and teach the Christian faith, as the scribes of Jesus' time studied and taught the Hebrew scriptures. The earliest writings that I discuss date from almost 500 years ago; even the latest are approaching 200 years of age. The writings are therefore old treasures.

The book is written out of my discovery as a reader that they are treasures indeed, comprehending a wealth of spiritual depth, intellectual acumen, and literary power. Those qualities do not fade or diminish with time. They are available to the modern reader who is willing to make the not very onerous adjustment to their language and historical context. The old writings thus become new treasures, in the minds and hearts of their readers. This seems to be the process that Jesus envisaged in his short parable of the scribes. It is also the experience of Christians when they read the Bible: it is an old treasure whose riches perennially renew themselves. John Henry Newman drew on Jesus' parable in embracing the inheritance of Catholic teaching: "I receive the Church as a messenger from Christ, rich in treasures old and new, rich with the accumulated wealth of ages."

The writers in this book are not, then, of merely antiquarian interest. The essential truths of Christianity do not change, though their expression varies. It is a matter of bringing back into the light writings that have fallen into shadows. The old books may have gathered dust, but the contents continue to speak directly and pointedly. Because of this quality, the continuing newness of their treasure, I quote extensively from all my writers, so that the reader may experience them as far as possible at first hand.[1]

This book traces, in a highly incomplete sampling, how Anglicanism defined itself in the first three centuries of its existence as a distinct branch of Christianity. Anglicanism did not emerge complete, just as the Christian church itself does not emerge complete in the New Testament. Many characteristics have emerged only over time, often in response to new historical conditions, and sometimes with conflict and schism along the way.

The book is not written out of theological expertise. It is an account of what one reader has discovered when re-opening some of the classics, or old treasures, of Anglicanism, writings from earlier centuries that have helped shape the church's identity and have given spiritual guidance and sustenance to its members. Such claim as the book may have to expertise derives from bringing to these writings my knowledge and experience as a scholar of English literature and cultural history. I hope that approach enables me to identify and communicate the power or the vividness or the cogency that make these writings classics, and to relate them to the historical contexts in which they appeared.

It is an advantage for my approach that Anglicanism is an especially literary form of Christianity (though it could be argued that it has been defined no less by its centuries of superb musical expression). Anglican thought and spirituality have often been expressed in language and forms that are richly wrought or intellectually arresting or emotionally satisfying. Poetry is the foremost example of Anglican literature in the service of religion, but the sermon, the manual of devotion or Christian living, and even the controversial tract or philosophical discourse, are all instances where writings combine a primarily religious purpose with distinction as literary texts. The foundations of all such writings, and of all Anglicanism, are the Bible, the authority for its teachings, and the Book of Common Prayer, the model for its worship. In their longest lasting versions, the King James Bible of 1611 and the Prayer Book of 1662, these books perform their function so successfully not least because of a language that is majestic, direct, and resonant. These qualities have made them classics of English literature and shaping forces in Anglophone culture.

Anglicanism can mean many things: that is a notorious and often bewildering fact about the church. The process of definition, which is still continuing and still contested, has resulted in markedly different forms of religious expression. As a resident of Sydney, I am conscious of one extreme in this diversity, since most churches in the Diocese of Sydney have in recent decades discarded almost all the external signs that are usually associated with Anglicanism. Paradoxically, this is a perfectly Anglican thing to do: Sydney Anglicans are again putting into effect the program of militant Protestant reform that was advocated by one grouping within the church from the outset and which that group succeeded in putting into effect throughout England in the 1640s and 1650s.

My own faith finds its home in a different stream of Anglicanism, one that embraces its Catholic character. This stream, too, has existed from the outset, and it too has attained its most impressive expression at particular historical junctures, one in the earlier seventeenth century and another in the mid-nineteenth century. Catholic Anglicanism emphasizes continuity with the earlier church. This includes the doctrinal inheritance of the "Fathers of the Church," the early Christian or Patristic writers of the first seven centuries. It also includes the inheritance of liturgical worship and ritual from the pre-Reformation church that was to some extent continued at the Reformation and to a greater extent reclaimed in the nineteenth century. The renewed impetus given to Catholic Anglicanism in the nineteenth century, beginning with the Oxford Movement in the 1830s, made it the pre-eminent stream of Anglicanism for 100 or more years.

This book is offered as a testimony to the intellectual and spiritual treasure of Catholic Anglicanism. It is written with the aim of informing the curious inquirer about this branch of our cultural heritage, and of deepening the faith of Catholic Anglicans by acquainting them more fully with their particular religious heritage. The book itself has no polemical intent, even if several of the writers it discusses certainly did. I have no wish to argue against other versions of Anglicanism or Christianity. It will be sufficient if this short volume can indicate what Catholic Anglicanism means to its adherents.[2]

It begins with foundational documents, the Book of Common Prayer and the King James Bible. In the sixteenth century, John Jewel and Richard Hooker vindicated the newly separated Church of England as a legitimate part of the church catholic. In the seventeenth and eighteenth centuries, George Herbert, Jeremy Taylor, and William Law wrote directly and challengingly about the Christian life and the profound apostolic commitment that it demands. This is a characteristic not always associated with Anglicanism, and it rewards closer attention. In the nineteenth century, John Keble, John Henry Newman, and other members of the Oxford Movement returned to the doctrine of the church, asserting the centrality of the church in Christian living.

The areas of interest emerging from my selection of writers are apparent from that summary. The doctrine of the church is first broached by Jewel and Hooker. While they defend the separation of the English from the Roman church and from other forms of Protestantism, they seek continuities as well as differences, above all its continuity with the Catholic nature of the church as stated in its creeds. This essential defence of Anglicanism was later revived by the Oxford Movement. But the church was no less beloved by Herbert, who contemplates its beauties and its vicissitudes in his poetry, and in his prose teaches himself to labour as its humble servant. Taylor in the 1650s writes for those deprived of the Book of Common Prayer and the ministrations of its church. Law, too, vindicates the spiritual integrity of the church in the face of what he regarded as mere political convenience. A similarly jealous guardianship of the church's spiritual status would later launch the Oxford Movement.

Anglicanism has needed to define and justify itself as a distinct church that took institutional form in the sixteenth century but traced its roots to the early church and retained some of the riches of the medieval church. Its literature is not, however, concerned exclusively with the doctrine of the church. It has taught also disciplines of individual devotion and spirituality, the imitation of Christ through a life of love, apostolic simplicity, and service. The leaders of the Oxford Movement, who exercised an extraordinary authority in their day, achieved it as much by their spiritual example, their very strict personal disciplines, as by their intellectual stature.

Anglican spirituality has cultivated a tradition of retirement. Herbert and Keble were both men of intellectual and social eminence, who thrived in the competitive academic communities of Cambridge and Oxford, but chose to assume the modest role of country parson. Taylor and Law were ordained priests (like all our other writers), but spent long periods with no formal church role at all, living privately with the support of wealthy patrons. Their retirement was not in the first instance voluntary: Taylor was expelled from his living in the bitter church conflicts of the 1640s; Law surrendered his when he found himself unable to swear an oath to the new royal house of Hanover in 1714. Even if they did not intentionally turn their back on their clerical careers, both men knew that their conscientious choices would have that effect. By an unsurprising paradox, withdrawal from the day-to-day business of their immediate society gave all these men the opportunity to write the books by which they vastly widened their readership and continue to communicate with later generations.

A commonality shared by Anglican writers is the high place accorded to reason in their religious discourse. At the beginning of Anglican intellectual tradition, Hooker gives the classic treatment of this faculty. He asserts the ability of reason to judge between truth and error—an ability without which his readers could not judge the merits of his own arguments. He asserts also the ability of reason to judge between good and evil, albeit with the unavoidable proviso that our will does not always follow where the judgement of reason leads.

The conviction that the faculty of human reason, instilled in us by God, and working in conjunction with free will, may carry us a good way along the path of Christian faith and morals will recur in Taylor and Law. It is a conviction that gives less emphasis to the Fall and the reign of sin than appears in much Protestant teaching. It will be less visible in the Tractarians, who are in reaction against rationalism. The leading Tractarians were, nonetheless, formidably learned Oxford dons. They used that learning to reinstate a fervent faith and piety in a church they believed to have become prosaically rational. The collaboration of reason and learning with faith and devotion manifests itself everywhere in the writers of this book, as it does throughout Anglican tradition.

As Anglicanism has made its own distinctive contribution to the Christian church, so its writers have contributed to major varieties or genres of Christian writing. Herbert's extraordinary versatility in his use of poetic forms and Keble's studious observation of the church year as a structuring principle for his major book of poetry continue the adaptation of secular poetic means to Christian purposes begun by the Latin poet Prudentius in the fourth century. Taylor and Keble provide examples of the sermon as a literary mode that speaks to both mind and heart, by expounding Scripture and applying it to the life of the hearers. "Sermons employed the forms of literature being poetic and lyrical as well as imaginative and speculative."[3] Law deploys the weaponry of satire and the impassioned *contemptus mundi*, or contempt for worldly concerns, modelled by ancient and medieval writers, as he calls his readers to discard the values of the everyday world and devote themselves wholly to the service of God. In teaching the soul how to approach death, Taylor and Law revive the medieval genre of the *ars moriendi*, the "art of dying," which shows how dying may be approached as an art or skill, perhaps the most important one for the Christian to master.

What follows is a very selective survey of its field. Among many more complete surveys is Paul Avis's impressive *Anglicanism and the Christian Church*.[4] The seventeenth century is studied in H. R. McAdoo's *Spirit of Anglicanism*.[5] An excellent study of the leading figures of the Oxford Movement and after is Geoffrey Rowell's *The Vision Glorious*.[6] In its sampling of key writers throughout the centuries, this book has a modest similarity to Rowan Williams's theologically profound *Anglican Identities*.[7]

Another kind of incompleteness that is glaringly visible to the 21st-century reader is the absence of women writers. It is easy but not entirely true to claim that this absence corresponds to the social history out of which Anglicanism grew. Women figure prominently among 19th-century hymn-writers, for example. Christina Rossetti, who does not appear in this book, is a better poet than one of her literary models, John Keble, who does. Historians are re-discovering and re-evaluating earlier women religious writers as well, though so far few who belong in the category of Catholic Anglicans.[8] The absence of women among the treasures recovered in this book is just one aspect of its severe selectiveness, but one that nevertheless merits notice and future redress.

Endnotes

[1] In quotations, spelling, the use of capital letters, and, on rare occasions, punctuation are modernized. For primary sources, that is, the main texts discussed, page references are not given, since they would be numerous and obtrusive, and most readers are not likely to pursue them. For secondary sources, that is, modern discussions of the texts and their contexts, references are given.

[2] Like most such labels, the term, "Catholic Anglicanism", is constructed after the event, a modern descriptor of a reality that is fully recognized only in historical hindsight, and from a particular perspective. As far as I know, none of the writers in this book used the term. But they would have all recognized, and they all largely embraced, what is meant by it. I have with some reluctance eschewed the term, "Anglo-Catholicism," which has had currency since the time of the Oxford Movement in the mid-nineteenth century. The terms have a subtly different emphasis. "Anglo-Catholicism" has in recent times become enmeshed in disputes about teachings on gender and sexuality, and I wish to avoid those associations, which distract from my approach.

[3] Keith A. Francis and William Gibson, eds, *The Oxford Handbook of the British Sermon 1689-1901* (Oxford: Oxford University Press, 2012), p. xv.

[4] First published 1989; revised and expanded edition, London and New York: T & T Clark, 2002.

[5] Subtitled *A Survey of Anglican Theological Method in the Seventeenth Century* (London: A. & C. Black, 1965).

[6] Subtitled *Themes and Personalities of the Catholic Revival in Anglicanism* (Oxford: Oxford University Press, 1983).

[7] London: Darton, Longman and Todd, 2004.

[8] An important study is: Erica Longfellow, *Women and Religious Writing in Early Modern England* (Cambridge: Cambridge University Press, 2009).

Further Reading

Stephen Neill, *Anglicanism*. Harmondsworth, M'sex: Penguin, 1958; Oxford: Oxford University Press, 1978.

John R. H. Moorman, *The Anglican Spiritual Tradition*. London: Darton, Longman and Todd, 1983.

John Booty, Jonathan Knight, and Stephen Sykes, eds, *The Study of Anglicanism*, revised edition. London: SPCK and Philadelphia: Fortress Press, 1998.

Paul Avis. *Anglicanism and the Christian Church*, revised and expanded edition. London and New York: T. & T. Clark, 2002.

W. L. Sachs, *The Transformation of Anglicanism*. Cambridge: Cambridge University Press, 2002.

Bruce Kaye, *Reinventing Anglicanism: a vision of confidence, community and engagement in Anglican Christianity*. Adelaide: Openbook, 2003; New York: Church Publishing, 2004.

1

The Book of Common Prayer

The Book of Common Prayer is not only a manual of worship; it is also the defining document of Anglicanism. This standing is acknowledged in the constitutions of the Anglican Church of Australia and the Anglican Church of Tanzania, the Church of Nigeria and the Episcopal Church in the USA, among many examples. It is also evident in the fact that when modern liturgical reforms have been introduced, the authorities have always allowed the Prayer Book to remain in use where there is a wish for it.

Anglicanism is not built on a foundation of systematic theology, like Aquinas's *Summa theologica* for Roman Catholics or Calvin's *Institutes of the Christian Religion* for the Reformed churches. The role of the Prayer Book means that Anglicanism defines itself through its worship. This relationship accords with the ancient and frequently quoted dictum, *lex orandi lex credendi*: the law of prayer is the law of belief; the way we pray expresses best the nature of our faith.

The Book of Common Prayer presents as an august and changeless thing and, indeed, it has changed very little since 1662. Nevertheless, it went through many changes before arriving at that final form. Those changes track the shifting balance between three forces in the early Church of England: the Catholic stream, the Protestant or reform stream, and Crown and Parliament. The last of these forces was in play because the Church of England was a state church, governed by Crown and Parliament as much as by bishops, which in England is still the case theoretically if not practically.

The oldest part of the book is the Litany, which was issued separately in 1544 when England went to war briefly with France. The emergency of war helps explain the mood of intense penitence and earnest petition that marks the Litany: "Remember not, Lord, our offences, nor the offences of our forefathers; neither take thou vengeance of our sins: Spare us, good Lord, spare thy people, whom thou hast redeemed with thy most precious blood, and be not angry with us for ever." The introduction of this Litany in English was the only change to the medieval Catholic rites made under King Henry VIII, who had seized organizational control of the English church in 1534 but made no theological changes. Next, in the six-year reign of Edward VI, in 1548, came the insertion of a group of English prayers into the Latin Mass, encouraging the congregation to take communion, and administering it in both kinds (both bread and wine, not bread only, as had been the medieval practice). Over these years prayer books in English for private use, known as primers, were issued. These primers included the canticles, such as the Te Deum and the Magnificat, in the translations that would later appear in the Prayer Book.

The first Book of Common Prayer appeared in 1549. Momentously, it was written entirely in English. It incorporated the materials just mentioned, and many others, which are summed up in its title:

> *The book of the common prayer* (that is, public prayer, the daily offices of Matins and Evensong, later named Morning and Evening Prayer);
>
> *and administration of the sacraments* (that is, the two sacraments recognized by the Anglican church as "generally necessary to salvation," baptism and the Eucharist, with the variable Scripture readings used in the Eucharist);
>
> *and other rites and ceremonies of the church* (confirmation, marriage, visitation of the sick, burial of the dead, and one or two more);
>
> *after the use of the Church of England* (from the first the Anglican church saw itself one unit within the wider Catholic church).

The 1662 book has a longer title, to accommodate elements that were

Title-page of the Book of Common Prayer, 1662. The book was issued with several different title-pages, of which this is one of the more elaborate. The architectural framework resembles the kind of reredos that began to appear in English churches at this period, often inscribed with the Ten Commandments, the Our Father, and the Apostles' Creed. In this copy, the correction to the seventh-last line of the main panel and the striking out of lines in the lower part follow the corrections of the commissioners who prepared a definitive text of the Prayer Book, to be kept in all English cathedrals and collegiate churches.

then printed with the Prayer Book but are not strictly part of it, the psalms (read at Morning and Evening Prayer) and the ordinal (the ceremonial for ordaining clergy).

The Prayer Book of 1549 is the most Catholic version. It was designed to minimize antagonism from a public long accustomed to the rites of the Roman Catholic church. The book draws on earlier Latin service books, on the suppressed experiments of Roman Catholic reformers like Cardinal Francisco de Quiñones in Spain and Archbishop Hermann von Wied of Cologne, and on Protestants like Martin Bucer at Strasbourg. Its Mass, which retains that name, has a long canon with a commemoration of the Blessed Virgin and prayer for the departed, as well as features like introit psalms and the Agnus Dei, all of which disappeared in later revisions. Stephen Gardiner, the Roman-leaning Bishop of Winchester, was able to maintain in a book of 1551 that this Prayer Book Mass was compatible with Roman Catholic doctrine.

By making such a public claim, Gardiner may have harmed his cause, because one year later the second Prayer Book of 1552 slashed and reshaped the 1549 Mass, removing all the features that Gardiner had approved. There is evidence that the 1549 book was always intended as a first step only on the path of Reformation; soon after it appeared Archbishop Cranmer began planning a second book, and asked for criticisms and suggestions from continental reformers who had taken refuge in England, Martin Bucer and Peter Martyr Vermigli, a rare Italian among the Protestant reformers, who had joined Bucer in Strasbourg.

The result was a "Lord's Supper," not a Mass, in which the altar is replaced by a table "in the body of the church, or in the chancel," and in which communicants do not receive the body and blood of Christ as a part of a sacrificial rite but bread and wine as part of a memorial rite. The role of music is reduced and vestments are restricted. There are, however, many small improvements in language.

All these changes became academic in 1553, when Queen Mary I ascended the throne, reintroduced Roman Catholicism, and abolished the second Prayer Book after it had been in use less than a year. Mary died childless after a five-year reign, and the throne passed to her half-sister, Queen Elizabeth I, whose reign of forty-five years restored political and religious stability. There are indications that Elizabeth's personal preference was to re-establish the church of her father, Henry VIII, traditional Catholicism but without pope and monasteries, or, failing that, to return to the first Prayer Book of 1549. But Mary's persecution had had the effect of strengthening Protestantism, and Elizabeth faced pressure to take a more Protestant direction, especially from men who, during Mary's reign, had gone into exile in leading Protestant centres like Geneva, and now returned to England.

The third Prayer Book of 1559 therefore could do no more than reproduce the 1552 book with a few significant changes. Administration of communion reinstates the words "the body" and "the blood of our Lord Jesus Christ …". A much discussed rubric appears to reinstate traditional vestments, but this was nowhere put into practice. In 1561, fifty-eight lesser feast days were reinstated in the calendar, which had been stripped back severely by both the earlier books, though there was still no provision for those feasts to be observed liturgically. Elizabeth also encouraged musical settings of the liturgy. Anglican church music flourished in her reign, with the careers of Thomas Tallis and William Byrd, Christopher Tye and William Morley. The church anthem is one of the conduits through which the language of the Prayer Book flows, since many Anglican anthems are musical settings of the psalms, collects, and gospels that appear in the book.

Extreme Protestants, or Puritans, objected not only to these developments but to other features of the Book of Common Prayer: signing with a cross in baptism, wearing a white surplice as a priestly vestment, kneeling for communion, giving a ring in marriage. These four ceremonial features would be a source of contention for a century to come. There were a number of attempts in Parliament to revise the Prayer Book in a Protestant direction, but these were promptly overruled by the Queen.

When King James I succeeded Queen Elizabeth in 1603, the Puritans hoped that the new king, brought up in the Calvinist Church of Scotland, would revise the Prayer Book to their satisfaction. James called a conference on religious policy, but his fourth Prayer Book of 1604 made only a few small concessions to Puritan requests. It also added a section on the sacraments to the Catechism, a prayer for the royal family to the Litany, and thanksgivings that are counterparts to the prayers for rain or fair weather or peace.

In the following decades of the seventeenth century there was widespread adaptation of the book to opposite purposes. Puritan clergy often refused to observe rubrics and ceremonies of which they disapproved. Metrical versions of the psalms and canticles were printed in many copies of the Prayer Book and were used instead of the official translations. Bishops were often willing to overlook such irregularities, though sometimes parishioners protested, showing that the Prayer Book had won allegiance from at least part of the population. In the other direction, a Catholic movement associated with Bishops Lancelot Andrewes, William Laud, and John Cosin reinstated the altar and its ornaments, used reverences such as bowing and genuflecting, and reattached the prayer of oblation to the prayer of consecration in the Communion service. This last change incorporated the Anglican doctrine of Eucharistic sacrifice into the liturgy, its expression having been made merely optional in 1552.

The Book of Common Prayer was abolished for a second time in 1645, now by a Parliament in which Puritans had gained control, and which also abolished the office of bishop. The Prayer Book was replaced by a Calvinist *Directory for the Public Worship of God*, with few set prayers, no liturgical calendar, no burial service. The Prayer Book nevertheless survived in private use, and sometimes in discreet public use. In their supposedly extempore prayers, some clergy would recite the Prayer Book, which was embedded in their memory. It is said that more than one Puritan congratulated a priest on "extempore" prayers that actually came from the despised Prayer Book.

After the Puritan régime collapsed fifteen years later, another Prayer Book conference was held, with the usual three forces pulling in the usual different directions. The Puritans argued against reintroducing the book at all, but they were now in a weak position. Some of the reinstated bishops, led by John Cosin and Matthew Wren, wanted a more Catholic Prayer Book, but these ideas were associated with the polarizing memory of William Laud, whose steps in this direction had helped precipitate civil war. After thirty years of religious conflict, the restored King Charles II, his Parliament, and the more pragmatic bishops, led by Gilbert Sheldon, were concerned to limit grievances on either side. They minimized change in either direction, as Queen Elizabeth had done for similar reasons.

The fifth Book of Common Prayer of 1662 emerged in a more Catholic form than the preceding three, but in a less Catholic form than most of the bishops wished. Divisions were still sharp enough that a thousand Puritan clergy were removed from their posts because they would not subscribe to the new book. Changes to rubrics introduced Catholic features that could not be accepted into the spoken text, for example, in the Communion, the title, "Prayer of Consecration," and the directions for handling the bread and the cup. Mention of the dead, if not exactly intercession for the dead, was introduced in the prayer for the church in the Communion service. Collects were revised and several prayers added, including the famous and splendid prayer "for all sorts and conditions of men" and a "general thanksgiving." Also added were prayers for use at sea, an indication of the commercial and imperial expansion of England that was beginning to take place, and a harbinger of the eventual global spread of Anglicanism. The language was slightly modernized and smoothed out—something that had been going on through all the versions, and that continued afterwards with modernizations of punctuation and spelling.

Since 1662, the tables for the date of Easter had to be revised when England tardily adopted the Gregorian calendar in 1751; the lessons at Morning and Evening Prayer were reordered a number of times; several state services were deleted, such as a thanksgiving for the overthrow of the Gunpowder Plot of 1605, and prayers commemorating the execution of King Charles I, which they tendentiously call his martyrdom. The Thirty-Nine Articles, an incomplete and somewhat eccentric collection of doctrinal statements, are now printed at the end of the Book of Common Prayer, but they were not in the book as passed by Parliament or as printed in 1662; they are included for convenience only.[1]

The Book of Common Prayer is indelibly associated with Thomas Cranmer (1489-1556), Archbishop of Canterbury when the first two versions of the book were issued, who no doubt had overall responsibility for compiling them. There is surprisingly little direct evidence for this role, though there is much indirect evidence. Not all the language of the Prayer Book services comes in fact from Cranmer. The famous prayers and thanksgivings added in 1662 lack Cranmer's concision but are sometimes mistakenly attributed to him; the Psalms come from the "Great Bible" of Henry VIII (1539); the epistles and gospels in the Communion service come from the King James Bible (1611). Much else is Cranmer's translation of the Latin services of the pre-Reformation church. He also had a few English models, such as the marriage service, which even before the Reformation had been conducted in English.

Nevertheless Cranmer does stamp his translations with a distinctive and masterly style. On the one hand his language is direct and concise; on the other hand it has dignity, even nobility. These two qualities work together characteristically in one magnificent sentence in the burial service, in which the mourners farewell the physical body in the stark language of the here-and-now and then, in the triumphant language of faith, almost see it transformed into a spiritual body:

> we therefore commit his body to the gound, earth to earth, ashes to ashes, dust to dust; in sure and certain hope of the Resurrection to eternal life, through our Lord Jesus Christ; who shall change our vile body, that it may be like unto his glorious body, according to his mighty working, whereby he is able to subdue all things to himself.

Cranmer's conciseness owes something to the simplicity of much New Testament Greek and to the terseness of the Latin liturgy. Sometimes the Prayer Book can sound dry or pedantic: "grant that they may both perceive and know what things they ought to do, and also may have grace and power faithfully to fulfil the same" (Collect for the First Sunday after Epiphany, translated from the Roman liturgy). There is even a certain bleakness: the Book of Common Prayer tends to speak the language of servants rather than sons or daughters, of unworthiness rather than joyfulness. When it rises to passages of fervour and passion, these often occur in connection with penitence. In the general confession of the Communion service the consciousness of our sins is overwhelming and our need for forgiveness desperate: "The remembrance of them is grievous unto us; The burden of them is intolerable. Have mercy upon us, Have mercy upon us, most merciful Father". Cranmer's urgency is an addition to his source, the Roman Catholic reformer Hermann von Wied.[2] The parallelisms and repetitions of the passage reflect the style of Hebrew poetry in the Psalms. The metrical regularity of the second sentence, three phrases each of six syllables, is one of the means by which the Prayer Book achieves emphasis and memorability.

Repetition can also express hope and transformation, as in the collect for the feast of St John Evangelist, where the word "light" recurs four times: "we beseech thee to cast thy bright beams of light upon thy Church, that it being enlightened by the doctrine of thy blessed Apostle and Evangelist Saint John may so walk in the light of thy truth, that it may at length attain to the light of everlasting life". The word "light" is echoed by the sound of the words "bright" and "life," creating a verbal dazzle, all the more striking since in England this feast falls in the darkest days of winter. This almost baroque style dates from the 1662 revision; the original collect in the Sarum missal, and Cranmer's original translation of 1549, are more restrained.

The Book of Common Prayer is a manual not only of worship but also of instruction; this is one reason why it is able to serve as a defining document for the Anglican church. As a Reformation teacher and pastor, Cranmer took advantage of English in place of Latin to educate his congregations in the liturgy and the faith. There are long doctrinal expositions, almost like sermons, in the marriage service, in the visitation of the sick, in the Communion service. These passages show that the Anglican Reformation was not built primarily on preaching but on teaching through liturgy: *lex orandi lex credendi*. The congregation spends much time listening to these expositions, but, even so, the Book of Common Prayer provides more congregational participation than did the Roman liturgy or most Reformation liturgies, albeit less than we expect nowadays. In fact, the Puritan delegates to the Prayer Book conference of 1661 objected that the book gave the congregation too much to say. They wished to remove the versicles and responses and the reading of psalm verses alternately by priest and people, considering "the people's part in public prayer to be only with silence and reverence to attend thereunto, and to declare their consent in the close, by saying Amen."

Recent scholarship on the Book of Common Prayer and recent biography of Cranmer have emphasized Cranmer's personal Protestantism,[3] and have argued or assumed that the Prayer Book must be read through that lens. But the Book of Common Prayer does not enforce a single theology; at key points the wording of the rites is open to different understandings, for example on the presence of Christ in the Eucharist, or on predestination in the burial service. To give a Catholic cast to the Prayer Book is not a perverse misreading. It is not Cranmer's personal book; its form has been produced by many forces, not least the political necessity of holding together people of diverse religious leanings in one church.

Endnotes

[1] The varied character of the Articles is analysed by Newman in Tract 82 of the Tracts for the Times: see pp. 140, 146.

[2] This aspect of the Book of Common Prayer is discussed fully by Isaac Williams in Tract 86 of the Tracts for the Times (see pp. 150-2).

[3] An authoritative example is Diarmaid MacCulloch, *Thomas Cranmer: A Life*, revised edn (New Haven and London: Yale University Press, 2017).

Further Reading

Francis Procter and Walter Howard Frere, eds, *A New History of the Book of Common Prayer*. London: Macmillan, 1901.

F. E. Brightman, *The English Rite: being a synopsis of the sources and revisions of the Book of Common Prayer*, 2 vols. London: Rivingtons, 1915. A simpler comparison between different versions is afforded by: Brian Cummings, ed., *The Book of Common Prayer: the texts of 1549, 1559, and 1662*. Oxford: Oxford University Press, 2013.

Geoffrey Cuming, *A History of Anglican Liturgy*, second edn. Basingstoke, Hants.: Palgrave Macmillan, 1982.

Cheslyn Jones, Edward Yarnold, SJ, Geoffrey Wainwright, and Paul Bradshaw, eds, *The Study of Liturgy*, revised edn. London: SPCK, 1992.

Geoffrey Wainwright and Karen B. Westerfield Tucker, eds, *The Oxford History of Christian Worship*. Oxford: Oxford University Press, 2005.

Charles Hefling and Cynthia Shattuck, eds, *The Oxford Guide to The Book of Common Prayer: a worldwide survey*. Oxford: Oxford University Press, 2006.

Diarmaid MacCulloch, *Thomas Cranmer: a life*. New Haven, Conn., 1996.

Title-page of the King James Bible in an edition dated 1634. The left half of the border depicts the tents and emblems of the twelve tribes of Israel; the right half depicts the twelve apostles. The twelve apostles established the church, as the twelve patriarchs originated the twelve tribes. The inner part depicts the four evangelists composing the four Gospels.

2

The King James Bible

If the Book of Common Prayer gives Anglicanism its distinctive stamp, it is the Bible on which the teachings of Anglicanism are based. The Thirty-Nine Articles declare that "whatsoever is not read therein, nor may be proved thereby, is not to be required . . . that it should be believed as an article of the faith."

For most of the history of Anglicanism, the Bible has meant the great English translation of 1611, known as the King James Version.[1] This translation has formed the basis of several modern editions, variously known as the American Standard Version or the English Standard Version, the Revised Standard Version or the New Revised Standard Version. The word, "standard", in all these titles indicates that they accord primacy to the King James Version, though they contain such revisions as their editors have believed necessary for modern readers. That belief usually underrates the ability of readers to adjust to the idiom of the King James Version. The directness and clarity of its language make it rarely difficult to understand, while its distance from everyday speech is a means, common to texts in many religions, of evoking the sacred or numinous.

The title page of the King James Version calls it *The Holy Bible . . . Newly translated out of the original tongues, and with the former translations diligently compared and revised, by His Majesty's special commandment*. Following through the phraseology of that title will explain much of the character of this great document of Anglicanism.

What are the "original tongues," and what problems would they have posed for the seventeenth-century scholars who produced the

King James Bible? What we call the Old Testament (or more respectfully the First Testament), and what Jews call the *Tanakh*, was originally composed in the Hebrew tongue, except a few chapters in the related tongue, Aramaic. Early Hebrew survives largely in the Old Testament alone, so there are few external linguistic checks to help us understand it. This was even more the case before the nineteenth century, when archaeology widened our knowledge through discovery of inscriptions and other linguistic remains. Even today there are 400 words that occur only once in the Old Testament and nowhere else, and whose meaning must therefore be deduced from their context or from parallels in other languages. Such *hapax legomena*, or "once-spoken words," are also a feature of the early form of ancient Greek in which the epic poems of Homer were written, where they present the same problems of interpretation.

Fortunately, there is another early version of the Old Testament, in the Greek tongue, made by the Jews of Alexandria in the third century BC. This version is called the Septuagint, because it is said to have been translated from Hebrew by a panel of seventy-two men in seventy-two days, and "seventy-two" in Latin is *septuaginta duo*. The Greek Old Testament includes fourteen books that are not included in the Hebrew scriptures, and are mostly of later composition. The King James Bible also included most of these books, but in the category of "Apocrypha," a word whose meaning shades from "hidden away," to "unknown authorship," to "spurious." In retaining the Apocrypha the King James Bible maintained Catholic tradition, which accepts these books, against Protestant teaching, which mostly rejects them. The Thirty-Nine Articles explain that "the Church doth read [them] for example of life and instruction of manners; but yet doth it not apply them to establish any doctrine." Since the nineteenth century the Apocryphal books have often disappeared from the King James Bible, apparently as a means of making the volume smaller and cheaper, but that exclusion was never the intention of King James's translators. These books are a loss, some being fine examples of Jewish wisdom literature, some carrying the history and legends of the Jewish people closer to the time of Jesus Christ, and thus contributing to the coherence of the two Testaments as a unity.

It is likely that the first language of Jesus Christ was Aramaic but that he also spoke Hebrew. The New Testament was originally in the Greek tongue, however. The Greek of both the Septuagint and the New Testament is called *koine*, the "common language" or *lingua franca*. It is a simplified version of classical Greek, and was widely spoken in the eastern Mediterranean for a thousand years. Unlike Biblical Hebrew, a large body of writing survives in this tongue, so there is ample context in which to understand the text of the New Testament. Compared to classical Greek, Biblical Greek has a limited vocabulary and a straightforward syntax, or sentence structure, which the King James Bible follows quite closely. Much of the sublime simplicity for which we correctly praise the King James Bible is therefore really a legacy of the original Greek, and to the translators' wise choice not to adapt the original style to idioms of their own time.

What were the "former translations" available to King James's scholars? They were not all English. One was the Latin translation of about AD 400, mostly by St Jerome, known as the Vulgate, from *versio vulgata*, "translation in common use," and long the only version of the Bible known in Western Christendom. Another was the German translation by Martin Luther, completed in 1534. Luther's vernacular translation resulted from the Reformation doctrine of the primacy of Scripture and the right of individual Christians to read it for themselves. That doctrine is connected with the rise of an individualist mercantile culture in the cities of Europe, which was challenging traditional power élites, including the clergy. The widespread reading of Scripture was made possible by printing and the book trade, innovations of that same mercantile class. There had been earlier translations, like John Wycliffe's in English in the late 1300s, but before the invention of printing they could not circulate widely. This was especially so because the Roman Catholic church long remained hostile to production of vernacular Bibles: in reaction to Wycliffe, translation was forbidden by English church authorities in 1408.

The person who defied that prohibition was William Tyndale (c1494-1536), educated at Oxford, where he must have learned Greek and possibly Hebrew, but where he disapproved of the new vogue for classical learning and formed the intention to produce a Bible in English. To do so he had to go to Germany, where his New Testament in English was published anonymously in 1526, shortly after Luther's German translation. Several editions followed, together with the beginning of an Old Testament. These books were at first smuggled into England, where they found an eager public. Tyndale continued to work on the Old Testament on the Continent, but he was executed for heresy by the Roman Catholic authorities of Antwerp in 1536. Tyndale's ambition, typical of the Reformation, was to "cause a boy who drives the plough to know more of the scriptures" than the priests of the unreformed church. Tyndale's translation is strongly Protestant: he translates *ecclesia* not as "church" but "congregation," and *presbyteros* not as "priest" but "senior."

Tyndale's is the most influential of the "former translations" that contributed to the King James Bible; it has been calculated that eighty per cent of the King James text can be traced back to Tyndale in the parts that he translated. This survival is a remarkable achievement when it is remembered that Tyndale was breaking new ground and that he worked largely single-handed.

Tyndale's work was completed by his collaborator, Miles Coverdale (1488-1569), who, in 1535, published the first complete Bible in English since Wycliffe. Coverdale made use of the Vulgate and Luther's translation, but not of the original Hebrew and Greek texts, so his contribution does not have high value as scholarship. It is, however, very good English: Coverdale's translation of the Psalms was incorporated into the first Book of Common Prayer, and it remains the version printed with the Book of Common Prayer. It is perhaps the smoothest and most mellifluous English version, and therefore best suited to chanting.

In 1537 there followed "Matthew's Bible," named from the pseudonym of its editor, John Rogers (c1505-1555), who carried on Tyndale's work in the dangerous setting of Spanish-ruled Antwerp (and eventually suffered execution back in England under Queen Mary I). This version makes use of Tyndale's unpublished parts of the Old Testament, supplemented by Coverdale. Matthew's Bible followed Luther in relegating to the end of the New Testament four books whose place in the canon Luther doubted (Hebrews, James, Jude, and Revelation); Matthew also introduced notes of a strongly Protestant character. Neither of these features was acceptable to the government of King Henry VIII. Therefore, in 1539, there appeared the Great Bible, edited by Coverdale, essentially a revision of Matthew's Bible with the customary order of the books restored and the offending notes removed. This was the first Bible authorized by the English monarch as head of the English church. Coverdale, Matthew, and the Great Bible are all similar translations, and appeared within five or six years of one another.

So matters stood for the rest of the reign of Henry VIII and for the short reign of King Edward VI. When Mary Tudor came to the throne in 1553 with a policy of reversing the Reformation, leading Protestants fled to the continent, many to Geneva, a centre of Protestant learning under the French exile, John Calvin. Led by an Oxford scholar, William Whittingham (c1524-1579), the English exiles completed a new translation in 1560. This "Geneva Bible" was the most widely read English translation for almost a century, during which it went through 140 printings, without ever being accorded official acceptance. It would take some decades for the King James Bible to overtake the Geneva Bible in circulation: that probably did not happen until after the Restoration in 1660. Tyndale's translation was again the basis for much of this Bible, but it made several innovations, some following the example of the great printer Robert Estienne, or Stephanus, another French exile in Geneva. It is not printed in old-fashioned black letter type but in the cleaner and clearer roman type that is still in general use. It divides the text into the numbered verses with which we are familiar. It has a convenient octavo format (230 mm tall), not the folio of Tyndale's successors (480 mm tall). The Geneva format is an indication that this Bible is for private rather than public use. Like Matthew's Bible, the Geneva Bible includes notes: there are introductions to each book, explanations in the margin, and also illustrations and maps. A tradition that urges individual interpretation thus paradoxically loads the text with its own interpretations.

The Geneva Bible prunes some of Matthew's excesses—it uses

"church" instead of "congregation"—but its notes are markedly Calvinist. In particular, the Geneva Bible echoes Calvin's critical attitude towards monarchy, flouting the doctrine of obedience to a divinely constituted political authority, meaning themselves, that was endlessly promulgated by the Tudors and Stuarts. The word, "tyrant", is said to occur 400 times in the Geneva Bible, but not once in the King James. The politics of the Geneva Bible attracted the hostility of royal authorities—rightly so from their point of view, because it is likely that the wide circulation of the Geneva Bible and its politics later contributed to the willingness of Parliament to overthrow the monarchy and execute King Charles I in the 1640s. In reaction to the Geneva Bible another official translation appeared in 1568, a somewhat hasty revision of the Great Bible, carried out mostly by the scholarly bishops of the Elizabethan church, working separately on different books. It was this Bishops' Bible that was mostly read in churches until the appearance of the King James Bible forty-three years later.

There was one more English translation: a New Testament produced by the now exiled Roman Catholics at Rheims in 1582, followed by an Old Testament at Douai, in northern France, in 1610. The Rheims-Douai Bible is translated from the Latin Vulgate, which the Council of Trent had declared the definitive version of the Bible. This dogmatic origin diminishes its scholarly value. Its translators did nevertheless make use of the original tongues, as the King James translators would, in their turn, make occasional use of the Rheims New Testament. The Douai Old Testament appeared too late to be consulted by those translators, however.

Thus, when King James VI of Scotland was proclaimed King James I of England in 1603, there was an official Anglican Bible challenged from the Calvinist side by the Geneva Bible and from the Roman side by the Rheims New Testament. These were the circumstances of "his Majesty's special commandment" for a new translation. The "special commandment" was issued as the result of a conference at Hampton Court Palace in 1604, convened by the King to bring together the mainstream church and the Puritan party, who regarded the English church as insufficiently reformed. In the event, the conference only alienated the Puritans further, since the King and the bishops accepted none of their requests or demands. But when a Puritan delegate criticized the Bible translations used by the Church of England, James seized the opportunity to suggest a new one. This gesture had the appearance of appeasing the Puritans; in fact, the new translation would aim to create a more credible alternative to the Geneva Bible, and thereby counter one of the Puritans' strongest weapons.

James himself had scholarly inclinations, so, as well as a political aim, he doubtless had the aim of giving the Church of England at last a full translation on a sound scholarly basis with which his name would be associated. As a matter of fact we do not have evidence that James was actively involved after his initial suggestion. The work was overseen by Richard Bancroft, Archbishop of Canterbury, an able and intransigent defender of the established church and the royal prerogative. Where the previous Anglican translations (as distinct from Geneva) had been one-man efforts or hurried revisions, Bancroft assembled a large body of translators, most of them impressively learned, whether in Hebrew and Greek or in Arabic, Syriac, and Ethiopic; a minority of Puritan scholars contributed.

Bancroft organized six "companies" of about eight members each, who worked together on six main divisions of the Bible, in the efficient manner of modern research collaborations. There were arrangements, probably not fully observed, for reviewing and cross-reviewing. This body of translators recalls the seventy-two translators of the Septuagint, and perhaps James and Bancroft intended a comparison with that model. Two companies worked in Oxford and two in Cambridge, both containing several professors and heads of colleges, and two worked at Westminster. Many notable scholars figured among James's translators. Lancelot Andrewes, at that time Bishop of Chichester, could read six ancient and fifteen modern languages; John Overall, Dean of St Paul's, habitually thought and wrote in Latin, to the extent that he found it difficult to preach in English.

Bancroft instructed his translators to work from the Hebrew and Greek originals, but to follow as far as possible the Bishops' Bible except where any of the earlier translations, including Geneva, was considered better. The King James Bible therefore builds on its predecessors; the preface says, "we never thought that we should need to make a new translation, nor yet to make of a bad one a good one, . . . but to make a good one better, or out of many good ones, one principal good one." This is partly a riposte to Puritan critics: the translators saw themselves as defending and extending an Anglican tradition of Biblical study that was already of high scholarly quality. Bancroft's instructions also ensured that the new translation avoided the Protestant excesses of Tyndale and the Geneva Bible: the opinions of the "ancient fathers"—and therefore of longstanding church tradition—were to be consulted, and "the old ecclesiastical words to be kept, . . . the word church not to be translated congregation . . . no marginal notes at all to be affixed." A surviving memoir gives a glimpse of James's company of formidable intellects sitting at a table, checking one another's work against a wide range of "former translations": "one read the translation [that he proposed], the rest holding in their hands some Bible, either of the learned languages, or French, Spanish, Italian, etc. If they found any fault, they spoke up; if not, he read on."

When first printed in 1611, the King James Bible, in common with what I have called its official predecessors, appeared in folio (though editions in smaller format soon followed). It was therefore in the first instance designed not for personal use but for a lectern, fulfilling, like its predecessors, Henry VIII's injunction of 1538 setting up a Bible in every church. The King James Bible likewise followed its official predecessors by reverting to black letter type, a dated choice by 1611.

The title page says that the new translation is "appointed to be read in churches," but that may mean no more than "suitable for reading in churches," because, strangely enough, there is no record that the new translation received explicit official authorization or recommendation from church or state. For that reason, the traditional name, "Authorized Version," has tended to fall out of use in recent times.

Archbishop Bancroft's direction to follow versions dating back eighty-five years gives the language of the King James Bible an old-fashioned cast, even in 1611. To take some characteristic verses: "Go, hide thee, thou and Jeremiah; and let no man know where ye be"; "The wind bloweth where it listeth, and thou hearest the sound thereof." The pronouns *thou*, *thee*, and *ye*, the verb endings of *hearest* and *bloweth*, had been standard English in Tyndale's day, but were disappearing around 1600. Probably Bancroft and the translators believed that this slightly archaic character was appropriate to their sacred text.

The King James Bible does not include interpretative notes. It does, however, assist the reader to navigate the text by a list of contents at the beginning of each chapter; these re-appear as headings at the top of each page. Like the Apocrypha, these useful aids often disappear in recent printings. They are presented as subject summaries, but they do occasionally shade into interpretation.[2] The edition also gives much concise information about the text. Words that are necessary in English but do not have a direct equivalent in Hebrew or Greek are printed in a different font. In the 𝔟𝔩𝔞𝔠𝔨-𝔩𝔢𝔱𝔱𝔢𝔯 original these words were printed in small roman; in later Bibles, printed in roman type, they are printed in *italic*. This is a feature that has puzzled most readers, and now has the unintended effect of making these words look more important rather than less, since in modern printing italics are usually employed for emphasis.

In the margins are cross-references to related passages. Together with the division by verses, this cross-referencing encourages an analytical approach, a comparison back and forth between small units of text; for better or worse, it tends to break up the consecutive reading that we practise in other books. The marginal notes also give alternative translations where there is linguistic doubt. Some feared that admitting doubt might undermine faith in the scriptures, but King James's scholar-clergymen believed it was their duty to give the most complete and accurate information at their disposal, and that included admitting to uncertainty. The Anglican confidence in the capabilities of the human mind here includes recognizing the limits of our knowledge. In its overall character, therefore, the Anglican King James Bible is less dogmatic, leaves more to the reader, than the Puritan Geneva Bible, and so is arguably more faithful to the scriptural mission of the Reformation.

Nevertheless, the King James Bible does have its own biases. Geneva's "tyrant" was replaced as a political codeword by "majesty," which appears seventy-two times in the text, and eighteen more times in the dedication and preface, to "the most high and mighty prince, James, by the Grace of God, King of Great Britain, France, and Ireland, defender of the Faith, etc." Earthly monarchy and "majesty" merge with divine monarchy and "majesty," in accordance with James's high view of himself and his office, and, in this way, the King James Bible is a fitting memorial to its patron.

Endnotes

[1] For the name "Authorized Version," see p. 28.

[2] A striking case arises with the Song of Solomon, a lavishly erotic love poem of a recognizable Middle Eastern type that found its way into the Hebrew scriptures. The chapter headings in the King James Bible describe the contents allegorically, a mode of interpretation that is applied to the book in both Jewish and Christian traditions. The verse, "Let him kiss me with the kisses of his mouth; for thy love is better than wine" (1:2) is explained as "The Church's love unto Christ." The passage, "Thy navel is like a round goblet, which wanteth not liquor . . . How fair and pleasant art thou, O love, for delights! This thy stature is like to a palm tree, and thy breasts to clusters of grapes" (7:2, 6-7), is explained as "A further description of the Church her graces [the Church's graces]."

Further Reading

Christopher Hill, *The English Bible and the Seventeenth-Century Revolution.* London: Allen Lane, 1993.

Alister E. McGrath, *In the Beginning: the story of the King James Bible and how it changed a nation, a language and a culture.* London: Hodder & Stoughton, and New York: Anchor Books, 2002.

Adam Nicolson, *Power and Glory: Jacobean England and the making of the King James Bible.* London: Harper Collins, 2003.

David Crystal, *Begat: the King James Bible and the English language.* Oxford: Oxford University Press, 2011.

David G. Burke, John F. Kutsko, and Philip H. Towner, eds, *The King James Version at 400: assessing its genius as Bible translation and its literary influence.* Atlanta GA: Society of Biblical Literature, 2013.

3

John Jewel

At a time when the Anglican church is in danger of splitting apart under the forces of conflicting theologies and ethics, we may take encouragement from the fact that the Anglican church still exists at all, because it has often been in danger of splitting apart, and has sometimes actually done so, most tragically in the English Civil War of the 1640s and '50s. Another perilous period came after 1558, when the new Queen Elizabeth re-established the church after the Roman Catholic régime of her half-sister Queen Mary. Elizabeth's settlement sought to strike a balance between the Protestant and Catholic sympathies that divided the kingdom. It wedded a generally Protestant statement of doctrine to a generally Catholic organization and liturgy, in the hope that everyone would find something they could accept and that a synthesis might gradually be achieved.

There was no certainty that that would happen but, in the first years and decades of the re-established Church of England, the synthesis was defended and developed by a number of writers, whose work helped clarify and solidify the church's self-definition. Among the most effective of these writers were John Jewel and Richard Hooker. They defended the Elizabethan settlement against criticism from two sides, Jewel against criticism from the church of Rome, Hooker against criticism from more extreme Protestants. Both their defences put a considerable emphasis on the Catholic claims of the English church. They thus laid the foundations of the Catholic Anglicanism that would be built upon by the seventeenth-century divines and their successors.

In the early stages of Elizabeth's settlement and its precarious balance, a new session of the Council of Trent was announced for 1562. Trent was Rome's response to the Reformation. The possibility that the English church might send representatives to the new session was actively considered in Rome and London. The possibility evaporated when Rome declared that submission to papal supremacy was a requirement for attendance, because the English church believed that papal supremacy was something that should itself be on the table for debate at a Council. In this impasse, "because we can by no means have audience in the public assembly of the general council, . . . we thought it good to yield up an account of our faith in writing." That is the explanation for the appearance in 1562 of *An Apology of the Church of England*, a declaration of the doctrine and historical claims of the English church. (The book is an "apology" in the original Greek sense of the word, a speech of defence in a law-court.)

The *Apology of the Church of England* did not carry the author's name: it presents itself not as the views of an individual but as a declaration by the English church as a whole. Its quasi-official character, as well as its enduring value as a statement of the English case, was made clear in 1609, when Archbishop Richard Bancroft ordered that every parish church should own a copy—and copies still survive here and there in English parish churches. We know that the author was John Jewel (1522-1571), a leading early reformer, exiled on the continent under Mary and appointed Bishop of Salisbury in the first round of episcopal appointments under Elizabeth.

The *Apology of the Church of England* appeared first in Latin, then in English, French, German, Italian, and Spanish. Through this book and its multiple translations the English church was appealing over the head of the Council of Trent and the pope to a wider readership, which it could reach thanks to the technology of printing. "I pray thee, whosoever thou be, read our books: they are to be sold in every place," Jewel writes. Printing and the Renaissance spread of commerce had given people access to the Bible and had therefore changed the patterns of intellectual authority, as Jewel astutely observed: "For the people of God are otherwise [differently] instructed now than they were in times past. . . . Nowadays the Holy Scripture is abroad, the writings of the apostles and prophets are in print, where-

John Jewel, from a 1685 edition of *An Apology of the Church of England*. This is the best of many engravings based on the sole contemporary portrait of Jewel, which is now in the National Portrait Gallery, London.

by all truth and Catholic doctrine may be proved, and all heresy may be disproved and confuted." Another sign of these changing times is that the English translator of the *Apology* was a woman, Anne Lady Bacon, mother of the philosopher of science, Francis Bacon.

The central claim of Jewel's *Apology* is that the faith of the English church rests on the authority of Scripture and on the traditions of the church. It is "confirmed by the words of Christ, by the writings of the apostles, by the testimonies of the Catholic Fathers, and by the examples of many ages." The *Apology* has a Biblical emphasis, as it should, and as we would expect from a reformer of Jewel's generation, but it also repeatedly calls on the early Fathers, the councils, and other witnesses from the history of the church. The English church may not be represented at the Council of Trent, but Jewel is eager to demonstrate that it derives from and maintains ancient Catholic tradition, more faithfully, indeed, than the sixteenth-century church of Rome.

The term, "Catholic", appears often in the *Apology*, more often than usually from a reformer of Jewel's generation. Jewel was undoubtedly a fervent Protestant, as were all the first generation of Elizabethan bishops, but he nevertheless defends the English church as both Reformed and Catholic. In doing so he lays the foundations on which later Catholic Anglicanism could build. The aim of the *Apology* is to "show it plainly that God's holy Gospel, the ancient bishops, and the primitive church do make on our side, and that we have . . . returned to the apostles and old Catholic fathers"; also that we "have directed, according to their customs and ordinances, not only our doctrine, but also the sacraments and the form of common prayer." The role of the Book of Common Prayer in defining Anglicanism is already apparent, as is the link between that book and Catholic tradition.

In a succinct summary of the beliefs of the English church, Jewel begins with the primacy of Scripture in establishing and confirming doctrine. In support of that primacy he quotes "the Catholic fathers and bishops" Augustine, Jerome, and Ambrose. For the government of the church, Jewel affirms the three orders of bishops, priests, and deacons. He quotes the Fathers Cyprian and Jerome to show that in the early church all bishops were equal, with no special status for the Bishop of Rome, and he quotes the Nicene Council's statement that the patriarchs of Alexandria and Antioch have equal status with the Bishop of Rome. He also makes the point, which is still valid, that it is impractical to centralize religious authority in a single person: "there can be no one mortal creature, which is able to comprehend or conceive in his mind the universal church, that is to wit, all the parts of the world, much less able rightly and duly to put them in order, and to govern them rightly and duly." Jewel defends the right of the clergy to marry, on which point he neatly finds support from a recent fifteenth-century pope: "For it was rightly said by Pius the Second, Bishop of Rome, 'that he saw many causes why wives should be taken away from priests, but that he saw many more, and more weighty causes why they ought to be restored them again.'"

The sacramental power of the clergy to bind and loose, to absolve sin, Jewel interprets in a less sacramental and more allegorical sense than in Catholic teaching: "touching the keys, wherewith they may either shut or open the kingdom of heaven, we with Chrysostom say, 'They be the knowledge of the Scriptures:' with Tertullian we say, 'They be the interpretation of the law:' and with Eusebius, we call them 'The Word of God.'" In true reformist fashion, Jewel insists that "the key whereby the way and entry to the kingdom of God is opened unto us, is the word of the Gospel." This interpretation suggests that the priest exists only to put people in possession of the key or to teach them the use of the key, that is, to preach the Gospel, but on a broader interpretation one could agree that it is through the truth of the Gospel, in conjunction with the Gospel, that the priest fulfils his office of forgiving sins. Word and sacrament function together; neither is subordinate to the other.

Jewel maintains a high doctrine of the Eucharist: "in the Lord's Supper there is truly given unto the believing the body and blood of the Lord, the flesh of the Son of God, which quickeneth our souls, . . . the food of immortality, grace, truth, and life." Jewel's Eucharist is no mere commemoration, as it is for most continental reformers. As Richard Hooker later does, Jewel insists on the reality of Christ's presence in the Eucharist. Jewel naturally insists on communion in both kinds and on celebrating the liturgy in the vernacular language, for which he appeals to Catholic precedent in emphatic terms: "for so both Christ hath commanded, and the apostles in every place have ordained, and all the ancient fathers and Catholic bishops have followed the same." These are points where the Roman church eventually instituted the same reforms as the English church.

A delicate question of doctrine arises when Jewel writes that Christ's body and blood are truly present "unto the believing." He explains, "it is our faith that applieth the death and cross of Christ to our benefit, and not the act of the massing priest. 'Faith had in the sacraments,' saith Augustine, 'doth justify, and not the sacraments.'" It can be argued that Jewel, and the Thirty-Nine Articles, maintain a "receptionist" doctrine of the Eucharist; it is only to the truly faithful communicant that Christ is really present. But it is noticeable that Jewel writes collectively, not individually: "our faith . . . our benefit . . . the believing [in general]." I understand him to mean that it is through the faith of the church as a whole, in conjunction with the church as itself the body of Christ, that Christ is present in the Eucharist; it is not just a private transaction with a faithful individual. "Look not on my sins but on the faith of thy church" was the prayer of the priest before his communion in the Roman Mass of Jewel's day. Likewise, the Book of Common Prayer joins the communicant to the greater body of the church, recognizing that "we are very members incorporate in the mystical body of thy Son, which is the blessed company of all faithful people."

After his summary of the leading doctrines of the English church, Jewel turns to a defence of the English church as an institution. He argues that the English church had good reason to separate itself from the Roman communion, and that in doing so it has retained a continuity with the church of the apostles, the early councils, and the early Fathers. In other words, the English church has maintained its Catholic character, in a purer form, Jewel claims, than the Roman church of his day. Is the English church a new invention? That would be a grave charge: "there can nothing be more spitefully spoken against the religion of God than to accuse it of novelty, as a new-come-up matter: for, as there can be no change in God himself, so ought there to be no change in his religion." The Roman church claims that it is the original and the English church a mere novelty. Jewel turns this claim around:

> But how if the things which these men are so desirous to have seem new be found of greatest antiquity? Contrariwise, how if all the things well nigh [i.e., almost all the things] which they so greatly set out with the name of antiquity... be at length found to be but new, and devised of very late?

Jewel shows that many of the doctrines and practices of the Roman church of his day are in this category. Celibacy of the clergy, communion in one kind, rejection of the vernacular in worship, discouragement of Bible reading, the granting of indulgences: none of these things can be traced to the church of the Fathers. In embracing them, the Roman church forfeits the marks of the true Catholic faith: "they have not that antiquity, they have not that universality, they have not that consent of all places, nor of all times." Jewel here paraphrases the formula of Vincent of Lérins in the fifth century: the Catholic faith is "what has been taught always, everywhere, and by all" (*Quod semper, quod ubique, quod ab omnibus traditum est*). The English church claims to maintain those ancient core Catholic doctrines.

It is possible to maintain that ancient faith while engaging in reform; in fact, writes Jewel, it is necessary to engage in periodic reform if we are to maintain the purity of the faith. Reform has occurred again and again among God's people. The prophets denounced the waywardness of the Jews; Christ condemned the abuses of the temple at Jerusalem; St Paul censured the churches of Galatia and Corinth. The Roman church itself has recognized the need for reform: Jewel here makes effective use of criticisms from within, by Bernard of Clairvaux in the eleventh century and by the Fourth Lateran Council in the thirteenth century. In Jewel's eloquent summary,

> the church, even as a corn-field, except it be eared, manured, tilled, and trimmed, instead of wheat it will bring forth thistles, darnel, and nettles. For this cause did God send ever among both prophets and apostles, and last of

all his "own Son," who might bring home the people into the right way, and repair anew the tottering church after she had erred.

The reform of the English church is another example of this necessary and God-inspired process; it is acting as the true church has always acted. From the Roman point of view there has been separation or departure, but Jewel takes a different perspective: "It is true, we have departed from them . . . But yet . . . from the primitive church, from the apostles, and from Christ we have not departed."

Jewel next considers the objection that reform can only be carried out by a council. Since the authority of councils is always respected in Catholic tradition and in Jewel's own argument, he must consider the authority of the Council of Trent. The problems for Jewel are: the Council of Trent will not hear the voice of reformers; it begins with the assumption that the Roman church cannot err, and therefore it does not entertain fundamental reforms; in the end it subordinates itself to the authority of the pope, so that it does not exercise the full powers of a council. The Council of Trent, Jewel shrewdly recognizes, has a pre-determined political purpose: to reaffirm the supremacy of the pope. It is right to absent oneself from such a council, writes Jewel, and he names early saints or churchmen—Athanasius, John Chrysostom, Cyril of Alexandria—who refused to attend councils that were politically motivated: "divers times many good men and Catholic bishops did tarry at home, and would not come when such councils were called, wherein men so apparently laboured to serve factions and to take parts, because they knew they should but lose their travail, and do no good."

Instead, the English church has introduced reforms by its own independent mechanisms. "[We] thought good to do the same thing, that both might rightly be done, and hath also many a time been done, as well of good men as of many Catholic bishops—that is, to remedy our own churches by a provincial synod." Jewel describes the legislation of Elizabeth's Parliament and the church convocation and debates that accompanied it: "The matter hath been treated in open Parliament with long consultation, and before a notable synod and convocation." In an impressive display of historical learning, he compares this procedure with a council of Carthage under Cyprian, a provincial synod called by Ambrose, councils called by Charlemagne, and also English precedents: "we have had ere now in England provincial synods, and governed our churches by home-made laws."

The patriotic note sounded here was always a feature of the English Reformation, but Jewel also takes a historical and geographical view of the church that is very broad. It is true that the English reform was not the work of a general council, but neither can Trent, nor even a council of the entire western church be a truly general or ecumenical council:

> For admit, peradventure, Italy, France, Spain, England, Germany, Denmark, and Scotland meet together, if there want Asia, Greece, Armenia, Persia, Media, Mesopotamia, Egypt, Ethiopia, India, and Mauritania, in all which places there be both many Christian men and also bishops, how can any man . . . think such a council to be a general council? or where so many parts of the world do lack how can they truly say they have the consent of the whole world?

The English church may have originated as the church of a single nation, but Jewel's *Apology* locates it in the wide geography and the long history of Christendom, with the aim of showing that it is part of that great Catholic totality.

Further Reading

W. M. Southgate, *John Jewel and the Problem of Doctrinal Authority.* Cambridge, Mass.: Harvard University Press, 1962.

J. E. Booty, *John Jewel as Apologist of the Church of England.* London: SPCK, 1963.

Alister E. McGrath, *Reformation Thought: an introduction*, second edn. Oxford: Blackwell, 1993.

Statue of Richard Hooker outside the cathedral of Exeter, his city of origin. There are no known likenesses of Hooker from his lifetime. This statue of 1907 by Alfred Drury (1856-1944) conveys pleasantly the ideal of a thoughtful and moderate scholar.

4

Richard Hooker

Reason and Revelation

John Jewel's *Apology of the Church of England* in 1582 defended the Catholic status of the English church against rejection by the Roman church. In 1594 the *Ecclesiastical Polity* of Richard Hooker (1554-1600) answered criticisms from the other side, the Puritans, who held that the English church was insufficiently Protestant, that reform needed to go further. The Puritans, whom we have encountered in earlier chapters, were so called because they sought to purify the church, to eliminate any traces of what they regarded as popery, but what others would regard as the church's Catholic character. Jewel and Hooker thus complement one another as they defend the English church against criticism from opposite directions. There was also a personal link between them. As Bishop of Salisbury, Jewel was impressed by the abilities of the young Hooker, thirty years his junior, and arranged for his education at Oxford. In return, Hooker praised, or over-praised, Jewel as "the worthiest divine that Christendom hath bred for the space of some hundreds of years."

Hooker's great work of 1594 has a formidable and unappealing title: *Of the Laws of Ecclesiastical Polity: Eight Books*. In modern terms, this title means that the book aims to establish the principles on which the church, or churches, should be organized and governed. In contrast to the hundred-odd succinct pages of Jewel's *Apology*, the modern scholarly edition of *Ecclesiastical Polity* runs to eight volumes. Hooker's work is more extensive in its subject-matter and more varied and human in its writing than the title suggests. Hooker can be amusingly ironical when answering his opponents;

he can be inspiringly rhapsodic when contemplating the works of God; he shows a charity towards other Christian confessions that is unhappily rare in Reformation controversy.

But Hooker is most remarkable for his qualities of mind, which take two main directions. First, he patiently constructs a magnificent intellectual edifice that can stand comparison in its power and originality with the great systematic treatises of Thomas Aquinas or John Calvin before him, of Thomas Hobbes or David Hume after him. Second, he exercises a lucid intelligence in analysing religious arguments. He states his principle of analysis with a typical clarity of thought and precision of language:

> The mixture of those things by speech which by nature are divided, is the mother of all error. To take away therefore that error which confusion breedeth, distinction is requisite. Rightly to distinguish is by conceit of mind [by the use of one's mental capacity] to sever things different in nature, and to discern wherein they differ.

Hooker is a master of the crucial distinction: what is divine law and what is human law? what is the authority of each? what are the essentials of faith and what are "things indifferent," where a variety of approaches or practices is allowable?

In answering the Puritan objections to the Elizabethan settlement of the English church, Hooker makes a number of arguments that are no longer of direct relevance. He shares the usual assumption of his day that there should be one sole church for the whole nation; that is no longer possible, nor even desirable. He therefore defends the union of church and state, with the sovereign as final authority in religious matters; that is likewise a union that few today would regard as possible or desirable.

But much in Hooker does have continuing interest. *Ecclesiastical Polity* was one of the first steps towards defining what would come to be recognized as Anglicanism; Hooker has even been called the inventor of Anglicanism. Part of his contribution was to emphasize the Catholic inheritance of the English church, as Jewel had done, and as both did to a degree unusual in English Reformation writers. Like the Elizabethan church that he was defending, Hooker combined Reformation and Catholic elements in his thought. There has been a recent trend among Protestant scholars to emphasize the Protestant side of Hooker and to deny the Catholic. A step towards redressing that imbalance is to consider Hooker's treatment of the sources of religious knowledge or wisdom, and how it relates to his vindication of Catholic tradition.

Among the various kinds of law that Hooker analyses, one is the law of reason:

> by force of the light of reason, wherewith God illuminateth every one which cometh into the world, men being enabled to know truth from falsehood, and good from evil, do thereby learn in many things what the will of God is; which will himself not revealing by any extraordinary means unto them, but they by natural discourse attaining the knowledge thereof.

For Hooker, God's gift of reason enables us to find out with our own natural human powers, apart from the teachings of Scripture, such things as God's existence or the principles of God's commandments—that is, the principles of ethics. Through the use of reason the pagan religions of the Greeks and Romans possessed a share in religious truth, "imprinted by the God of nature in their hearts also." Presumably Hooker would have extended this share to other world religions also, but they were largely unknown in Elizabethan England.

The law of reason is called a law in the sense of a scientific law: it enables us to recognize the way things are; through the law of reason we all recognize truths like "the greater good is to be chosen before the less" or principles like "do unto others as you would have them do unto you." Reason for Hooker is not a mechanical computer-like capacity; it is what we can learn or intuit through our human nature. Reason therefore takes in our whole way of seeing and thinking, our understanding and judgement, sometimes also our sympathy and feeling. We can, then, attain to a significant level of religious awareness even without the teaching of Scripture: Hooker is emphatic on this point and makes it a central feature of his argument.

Nevertheless, Scripture does impart a further essential kind of knowledge, which we cannot arrive at by reason. Here we come to another kind of law, divine law:

> concerning that faith, hope, and charity, without which there can be no salvation, was there ever any mention made saving only in that law which God himself hath from heaven revealed? . . . Laws therefore concerning these things are supernatural, . . . by the voluntary appointment of God ordained besides the course of nature, to rectify nature's obliquity [propensity to mislead].

We cannot attain salvation by our own natural reason or virtue; to do that we must obey the law of faith, hope, and charity laid down in Scripture: "The light of nature is never able to find out any way of obtaining the reward of bliss, but by performing exactly the duties and works of righteousness." ("The duties and works of righteousness": Hooker does not speak the language of a narrowly defined "justification by faith.") This second divine law, through which we attain salvation, is law in the legislative sense, or what is technically called positive law, rules of conduct laid down by an authority.

Scripture is essential to the work of salvation, but Hooker also asserts the dignity and the power of reason, that is, of our human nature; reason and revelation work together. Hooker compares the relation between the two laws to the relation between the Old Testament and the New: the Old Testament teaches that salvation will come, the New Testament that it has come; the Old Testament must be completed by the New. In the same way, reason must be completed by revelation, but the light of reason is not eclipsed by the light of revelation: "our own words . . ., when we extol the complete sufficiency of the whole entire body of the Scripture, must . . . be understood with this caution, that the benefit of nature's light be not thought excluded as unnecessary, because the necessity of a diviner light is magnified." Our natural understanding and Scripture work together, "both jointly and not severally," to supply all "needful instruction unto any good work which God himself requireth."

Why is this double source of religious knowledge important? For many reasons, one of which is often overlooked: "Scripture indeed teacheth things above nature, things which our reason by itself could not reach unto. Yet those things also we believe, knowing by reason that the Scripture is the word of God." When we accept the authority of Scripture, we do so on the basis of a choice guided by reason. The exercise of our reason is a pre-condition to our acceptance of Scripture, since the truth of Scripture is not self-evident, as a proposition like "the greater good is to be chosen before the less" is self-evident. If it were, it would be universally accepted. Scripture contains

> all things which are necessary to be known that we may be saved; but known with presupposal of knowledge concerning certain principles whereof it receiveth us already persuaded ... In the number of these principles one is the sacred authority of Scripture. Being therefore persuaded by other means that these Scriptures are the oracles of God, themselves do teach us the rest.

Certainly the Holy Spirit also has a part in our embracing Scripture; we will not find truth "if the special grace of the Holy Ghost concur not to the enlightening of our minds." But the Spirit, too, works through, or in cooperation with, reason. Otherwise, asks Hooker, how could we ever teach the Gospel to non-believers? To people who do not already believe in the Holy Spirit, it will not be enough simply to say this is what the Holy Spirit teaches; we have to persuade through reasons and evidence and probabilities and coherence, as the apostles and the early Fathers did.

Another function of reason, even in the realm of the spirit, is to serve as a check on the working of the Holy Spirit in ourselves: "it needeth caution and explication how the testimony of the Spirit may be discerned ... lest men think that the Spirit of God doth testify those things which the spirit of error suggesteth." It is unwise to leap into actions in the belief that we are moved by the Spirit, for we may be deluding ourselves. Since we cannot hope to predict or understand with any certainty the working of the Spirit, the wiser course is to make our choices through reason and then to discern from the results how the Spirit may have directed us.

The work of reason and the understanding of Scripture are not, for Hooker, private or solitary matters. This fact occasions the role of the church. It is through God's church that we learn of the existence of Scripture in the first place, and it is by the teaching of the church that we are led to the understanding of Scripture: "The Scripture could not teach us the things that are of God, unless we did credit men who have taught us that the words of Scripture do signify those things." In questions where there is no undoubted proof from Scripture or from reason we should follow what "a number of the learnedest divines in the world have ever thought"—in other words, we should follow Catholic tradition.

The laws of the church deserve the highest respect: "It doth not stand with the duty which we owe to our heavenly Father, that to the ordinances of our mother the church we should show ourselves disobedient." Since God is ultimately the author even of heathen laws, when they are made according to nature and reason, "How much more then is he the author of those laws, which have been made by his saints, endued further with the heavenly grace of his Spirit." Hooker sets this authority of the church against the extremes of individual judgement claimed by some Protestants, even, as he notes with measured scorn, those who are thoroughly ignorant: "a man whose capacity will scarce serve him to utter five words in sensible manner blusheth not . . . concerning matter of Scripture to think his own bare Yea as good as the Nay of all the wise, grave, and learned judgements that are in the whole world."

Nevertheless, authority must never lead to "a captivity of judgement": the simplest person, if he has reason on his side, must prevail even over "companies of learned men," just as any manifest teaching of Scripture or any demonstrable reason will overweigh "ten thousand general councils." Hooker views most aspects of church order and practice as "things indifferent," matters of convenience only, not matters of faith. Church traditions are to be respected, but they are not immutable unless directly supported by Scripture or reason. What is essential and immutable are "the public religious duties of the church, as the administration of the word and sacraments, prayers, spiritual censures, and the like"; what is changeable are "laws which appoint in what manner these duties shall be performed." Nevertheless, as will be shown in the second part of this chapter, Hooker is reluctant in practice to set aside what has been established by church tradition.

Hooker's answer to the Puritans builds on all the foregoing principles. The key issue is the Puritan insistence that Scripture only must be the law for all personal actions and for all aspects of the life of the church. Hooker accepts the rule of Scripture in the realm of doctrine and of moral actions, "which have in them vice or virtue," but he affirms his usual position that, for other actions and practices, "it sufficeth if such actions be framed according to the law of reason," and also to some extent following the precedent of church tradition, in cases where it is applicable. To glorify God it is not necessary to refer every action to some scriptural text, because Scripture is not God's only law; the law of reason and the law of nature, the laws of Christian rulers and the laws of the Christian church, all are aspects of God's law, "nor is there any law of God, whereunto he doth not account our obedience his glory."

Hooker therefore presents an idea of our relation to God that is broader, more generous, more catholic (in the primary sense of the word), than the exclusively Biblical idea of Puritan Protestantism. He also demonstrates, using impressive skills of textual and historical analysis, that the Calvinist model for church discipline favoured by the English Puritans actually has only a vague and unconvincing Biblical basis.

To put his argument in a yet broader historical perspective, Hooker writes in opposition to the whole thrust of the Calvinism that had strong support in the Elizabethan church. For Calvin, the fact of the Fall, the inheritance of original sin, meant that our reason is inadequate and our will treacherous. Calvin says: "whatever knowledge and understanding a man has . . . is of no more value for grasping spiritual teaching than the eye of a blind man for distinguishing colours." Hooker, by contrast, puts a high value on human knowledge and understanding, as a significant though incomplete means of achieving spiritual wisdom. Calvin says: "When the will is enchained as the slave of sin, it cannot make a movement toward goodness, far less steadily pursue it." Hooker knows that our will does not always obey our reason, but he does not view it as profoundly corrupted. While he acknowledges the fact that we are fallen, that fact does not dominate his understanding of human nature. Hence the phrase quoted above, "nature's obliquity": our world does not run quite straight, but it is not totally and irreparably damaged.

These assumptions associate Hooker with the Catholic inclusiveness of Aquinas and Erasmus. Aquinas, too, taught that there are two sources of knowledge, revelation and reason. For Aquinas, reason is embodied not only in the individual but also in ancient philosophers, especially Aristotle. Hooker shows allegiance to the same range of authorities: his most common authority by far is Scripture, but he also quotes the early councils and the early Fathers (especially Augustine and Tertullian), and he draws on the wisdom of non-Christian writers, especially Aristotle, Cicero, and Seneca, and even occasionally the poets Homer and Euripides. He rarely quotes Calvin or Luther or the other reformers.

In many ways, Hooker speaks out of a different world from ours, but there is also much that makes him worth listening to in our secular world, as in his sectarian world. One is his respect for human reason, our God-given capacity for understanding and connecting. Another is his broadening of religious discourse beyond a narrow commitment to Scripture and nothing more. These are things that make Hooker the spiritual father of a liberal Catholic Anglicanism.

Hooker and the Church

Hooker's contribution to laying the foundations of a Catholic Anglicanism extends beyond the matters of large-scale principle discussed so far, into the detail of religious practice. A starting-point for this subject is his view about the nature and purpose of ceremony. In the ministrations of the church, Hooker writes, we can distinguish between "that matter and form wherein the essence thereof consisteth" and "a certain outward fashion whereby the same is in decent sort administered." For the sacraments, "the essence" is the material substances (water, bread, wine) and brief verbal statements; that is all we find in Scripture. Administering those sacraments, the "outward forms," "doth require a great deal more," which must be supplied by human choice. What principles should we look to, what purpose should we aim at, when we administer them?

First, writes Hooker, to edify the church; that is, to work on the understanding and the feelings in such a way as to stir up attention, reverence, devotion. This is done not only through speech, which is all the Puritans allow, but also through sight. All nations give visual solemnity to public actions, including sacred or spiritual actions; "sensible actions" (that is, things that appeal to our senses) are more effective than words in moving our feelings.

Second, the ceremonies of the church should aim for a beauty that reflects the beauty of God, or the beauty of holiness, not only to instruct us, but for its own sake, or for God's sake. Ceremonies should have "a sensible excellency, correspondent to the majesty of him whom we worship" so that "the militant church doth resemble by sensible means . . . that hidden dignity and glory wherewith the church triumphant in heaven is beautified." Third, ceremony expresses outwardly our inward religious feelings, such as our aspiration toward the beauties of heaven.

As well as having these uses, ceremonies are the inheritance of the church, which it is our duty to maintain: "Neither may we . . . lightly esteem what hath been allowed as fit in the judgement of antiquity, and by the long continued practice of the whole church." The Puritans insisted that the English church should confine itself to the extreme simplicity with which the early church worshipped. Hooker points out that, to begin with, we have only partial knowledge of the early church and its style of worship; we should not erect general principles on such an uncertain foundation. Moreover, the Puritans ignore the fact that the earliest practices were produced by the historical conditions of a church in its infancy and under threat; they are not necessarily a pattern for later times. The Jewish people had very different styles of religious expression at different stages of their history. They worshipped simply when exiled in Egypt, with "greater compass" in Canaan, and magnificently in Solomon's temple in Jerusalem. God will accept praise in all forms, praise expressed with the "greatness and dignity of later times" as well as with "the reverend simplicity of ancienter times."

The Puritans rejected the chanting of psalms and the use of any musical instruments, including the organ; Hooker advocates the richer musical tradition that was being developed in his own time by the great Elizabethan school of church composers. Hooker points out that King David himself added "melody both vocal and instrumental" to his psalms. Summarizing Plato, he also points out that "so pleasing effects [harmony] hath in that very part of man which is most divine, that some have been thereby induced to think that the soul itself by nature is or hath in it harmony." He gives an eloquent description of the "admirable facility which music hath to express and represent to the mind, more inwardly than any other sensible means, the very standing, rising, and falling, the very steps and inflections every way, the turns and varieties of all passions whereunto the mind is subject."

In all these ways Hooker lays down the principles for a style of worship that differs from Puritan austerity. His principles assume the use of consecrated places of worship such as had already long existed in the church. Hooker is therefore amazed to find that he must defend even the existence of church buildings and their decoration, "the overthrow and ruin whereof is desired, not now by infidels, pagans, or Turks, but by a special refined set of Christian believers." Those believers are the Puritans again, whose modern successors are still discarding outmoded consecrated churches in favour of "contemporary worship spaces."

The sacraments, like ceremonies of all kinds, give visual expression to the unseen:

> sith [since] God in himself is invisible and cannot by us be discerned working, therefore when it seemeth good in the eyes of his heavenly wisdom, that men for some special intent and purpose should take notice of his glorious presence, he giveth them some plain and sensible token whereby to know what they cannot see.

To this end, God appeared as a burning bush to Moses, his angel stirred the pool of Bethesda, and the Holy Spirit appeared to the Apostles as fiery tongues.

But the sacraments, the most sacred and most efficacious of all ceremonies, are not merely the expressions but the actual containers of a sacred reality:

> For we take not baptism nor the eucharist for bare resemblances or memorials of things absent, neither for naked signs and testimonies assuring us of grace received before, but (as they are indeed and in verity) for means effectual whereby God when we take the sacraments delivereth into our hands that grace available unto eternal life, which grace the sacraments represent or signify.

This summary is in contrast to the teachings of continental Protestantism and lays the foundations of the sacramental theology of Catholic Anglicanism, which are evident also in Hooker's conviction that "sacraments are in their place no less required than belief itself."

Hence arises the importance of baptism, "the door of our actual entrance into God's house, the first apparent beginning of life, a seal perhaps to the grace of election, before received, but to our sanctification here a step that hath not any before it." Calvin, in the *Institutes of the Christian Religion*, had written that baptism is "only the seal of the grace of God before received." For Calvin, God either has or has not chosen you; baptism can do no more than stamp a seal on that pre-existing choice. Hooker gives one of his rare quotations from Calvin, to signal a disagreement (or at least a divergence). Against the purely conceptual doctrine of election Hooker emphasizes the actual, the experience of life, the process of "sanctification," in which the sacraments play a vital part. Logically, baptism may be no more than "a [mere] seal perhaps to the grace of Election, before received" but "to our sanctification here," to the journey of life as we live it, it has the freshness and wonder of a dramatic new beginning, "a step that hath not any before it."

For all his formidable intellect, Hooker is no mere theoretician; his priority is how we live out the Christian faith. He places that experience ahead of doctrines like election or justification by faith, which always run the risk of becoming self-satisfied. For this reason he compares dogmatic Protestants with the followers of Valentinus in the second century, who believed that redemption was achieved through "knowledge only": "They draw very near unto this error, who fixing wholly their minds on the known necessity of faith imagine that nothing but faith is necessary for the attainment of grace."

On the Eucharist, Hooker takes a high view of the presence of Christ in the sacrament, seen also in Jewel. Christ's "flesh is meat and his blood drink, not by surmised imagination but truly"; we attain "the real participation of Christ and of life in his body and blood by means of this sacrament." Related to his sacramental emphasis, Hooker holds a Catholic doctrine of the priesthood, deriving it from Christ's breathing on the apostles and his words, "Receive the Holy Ghost." Therefore, he writes, regarding the priestly function, "Whether we preach, pray, baptize, communicate, condemn, give absolution, or whatsoever, . . . our words, judgements, acts and deeds, are not ours but the Holy Ghost's."

Christ's commission included preaching the Gospel to all nations. Hooker interprets this activity in a broader way than the Puritans, who were, and are, the great exponents of the sermon. For, writes Hooker, "Sermons are not the only preaching which doth save souls." The English church offers a large body of Scriptural readings, especially in its daily offices of Morning and Evening Prayer. What is this but preaching? asks Hooker.

> Moses and the prophets, Christ and his apostles, were in their times all preachers of God's truth; some by word, some by writing, some by both . . . The church in like case preacheth still, first publishing . . . the truth . . . as it was received, written in the sacred volumes of Scripture; secondly by way of explication.

To be sure, understanding Scripture is not a simple matter: "as every thing of price, so this doth require travail." In this labour we benefit from the help of other men's judgements. That help may be given publicly, "which we call preaching," but it can also be given privately, and that can instruct and aid us just as much as sermons.

Hooker does not underrate sermons. In a beautiful rhetorical passage he praises them "as keys to the kingdom of heaven, as wings to the soul, as spurs to the good affections of man, unto the sound and healthy as food, as physic unto diseased minds." Nevertheless the Puritans are apt to entertain a "superstitious conceit [idea]" of the value of the sermon. They sometimes appear to think that the Scriptures were written only to give the preacher a text to comment on—that the gospel was made for the preacher, not the preacher for the gospel.

A leading aim of the Puritans was to purify the church from any traces of what they called popery. In his opposition to this programme, Hooker defends the continuity of the English church with earlier churches, including the Roman Catholic church. Using an argument that recalls the *pietas* of the ancient Romans, Hooker associates respect for religious tradition with respect for our own forebears. The English church has done right to retain "the ancient rites and customs of the church of Christ, whereof ourselves being a part, we have the self-same interest in them which our fathers before us had." Even if we have borrowed from the Roman church, is that so shameful?

> Doth the reputation of one church stand by saying unto another, "I need thee not"? . . . To say that in nothing they may be followed which are of the church of Rome were violent and extreme. . . . As far as they follow reason and truth, we fear not to tread the self-same steps wherein they have gone, and to be their followers.

Why then did the Church of England "alter her received laws concerning . . . orders, rites, and ceremonies"? Such change must be made only cautiously, especially when it comes to the laws of religion. Hooker, the legal theorist, is well aware that if laws are seen to be changed lightly, men will call into question whether any laws are valid or whether they are not merely preferences, "such as men at this or that time agree to account of them." That is because much of the authority of law rests on long agreement, "the weight of so many men's judgement as have with deliberate advice assented thereunto; to tread the weight of that long experience, which the world hath had thereof."

The English reform therefore kept changes to a minimum and removed only later accretions, such as the excessive number of saints' days; it did not remove things deeply rooted, which had been to alter unnecessarily . . . the ancient received custom of the whole church, the universal practice of the people of God, and those very decrees of our fathers, which were not only set down by agreement of general councils, but had accordingly been put in ure [use] and so continued in use till that very time present.

"Ancient custom," "universal practice": Hooker himself does not use the term, but he is invoking the concept of the Catholic faith as "what has been believed everywhere, always, and by all."

In his comparisons of the English church with the Roman church and with the demands of the Puritan reformers, Hooker signals that the English church is following a middle way, its famous *via media*, though Hooker does not use that term either. The need to find a median is implied when Hooker explains how the Roman communion has over-loaded the church, while the Calvinists have stripped it too bare:

Our dislike of them, by whom too much heretofore hath been attributed unto the church, is grown to an error on the contrary hand; so that now from the church of God too much is derogated. By which removal of one extremity with another, the world seeking to procure a remedy, hath purchased a mere exchange of the evil which before was felt.

That is to say, in some places the Reformation had swung from one unacceptable extreme to another.

In contrast, Hooker gives an instructive analysis of the middle way, showing that it is not a mere averaging out, a cautious half-measure, but a clear and strong alternative to both extremes:

we are not simply to measure good by distance from evil, because one vice may . . . be more opposite to another than either of them to that virtue which holdeth the mean between them. . . . The liberal-hearted man is by the opinion of the prodigal miserable, and by the judgement of the miserable lavish; impiety for the most part upbraideth religion as superstitious, which superstition often accuseth

> as impious, both so conceiving thereof because it doth seem more to participate each extreme, than one extreme doth another, and is by consequent less contrary to either of them than they mutually between themselves.[1]

That knotty passage is saying, first, that to depart as far as possible from one vice runs the risk of leading you not into virtue but into the opposite vice. Second, it is saying that if two opposite extremes both think you are wrong, then you are probably right. If the extravagant person thinks you tight-fisted and the tight-fisted person thinks you extravagant, then you are showing the correct balance of generosity and prudence; if the atheist thinks you superstitious and the superstitious person thinks you an atheist, then your religion is probably right. The correct choice lies in the middle; the extremes are so concerned to be opposite to one another that they both fall into error. If the Romans think we are too Protestant and the Protestants think we are too Roman, then we are probably in the right place.

Hooker believes that it is God who has guided the English nation into this middle way, restraining it from the extremes of Reformation that had caused such tragedy in other parts of Europe:

> the Almighty, . . . foreseeing . . . what tragedies the attempt of so extreme alteration would raise in some parts of the Christian world, did for the endless good of his church . . . use the bridle of his provident restraining hand, to stay those eager affections in some, and to settle their resolution upon a course more calm and moderate.

When matters are pushed to such "desperate extremities" that the outcome seems to entail "the utter oppression and clean extinguishment of one side," then the outcome will be violence, because under such extreme threat men will be driven to defend themselves and their beliefs through such measures as the "mutual combustions, bloodsheds, and wastes" that were taking place in the Netherlands and France when Hooker was writing. That being so, Hooker advises that "suspense of judgement and exercise of charity were safer and seemlier for Christian men, than the hot pursuit of . . . controversies." This is good advice now as then. Instead of enforcing our beliefs or preferences with intolerant zeal, counsels Hooker, let us wait on God's judgement: "who are on his side, and who against him, our Lord in his good time shall reveal."

The Elizabethan compromise that Jewel justified in its earliest stages has come to seem to Hooker, thirty or forty years later, to be the result of providential guidance. In Hooker's day, as in ours, there were powerful and threatening tensions within the English church. For Hooker, as for us, "our manifold sins and transgressions [were] striving to the contrary," threatening the unity that is Christ's wish. The English church had nevertheless survived and in some ways thrived: like Hooker we can draw the hopeful lesson that God permits its travails in order to prove to the world his care for it: "what can we less thereupon conclude, than that God would . . . by tract of time teach the world, that the thing which he blesseth, defendeth, keepeth so strangely [i.e., against all the odds], cannot choose but be of him?"

Endnotes

[1] With Hooker's treatment of the *via media*, compare that of the Oxford Movement, pp. 152-4.

Further Reading

W. Speed Hill, gen. ed., *The Folger Library Edition of the Works of Richard Hooker*, 7 vols in 8. Cambridge Mass., and London: Belknap Press of Harvard University Press; Binghamton, N.Y., and Tempe, Ariz.: Medieval and Renaissance Texts and Studies, 1977-98.

F. C. Beiser, *The Sovereignty of Reason: the defense of rationality in the early English Enlightenment*. Princeton: Princeton University Press, 1996.

A. S. McGrade, ed., *Richard Hooker and the Construction of Christian Community*. Tempe, Ariz.: Medieval and Renaissance Texts and Studies, 1997.

Christopher Morris, *Political Thought in England: Tyndale to Hooker*. London: Oxford University Press, 1953.

Nigel Voak, *Richard Hooker and Reformed Theology: a study of reason, will, and grace*. Oxford: Oxford University Press, 2003.

5

George Herbert

George Herbert is a leading light in the galaxy of seventeenth-century Anglican poets. He writes in lyric forms of great variety and inventiveness, and in the vigorous and startling style loosely called "metaphysical," which in his case is modified by an everyday homeliness. These qualities have won his poetry a continuing public far beyond religiously disposed readers. In prose, Herbert's manual of priestly duty, *The Country Parson*, still lives as a prized example of Anglican spirituality. His writings are among the most cherished treasures with which Anglicanism has endowed the English-speaking world.

Herbert was born in 1593, into a family whose great abilities were furthered by its aristocratic connections. The very grand Earls of Pembroke were George's distant cousins. His older brother, Edward, inherited the title, Lord Herbert of Cherbury, and became a diplomat, philosopher, and poet of some note. His younger brother Henry became Master of the Revels, an important officer in the Stuart court and in the history of English drama, since his licence was required to perform any play in public. Their mother, Magdelene Herbert, was the friend of John Donne, the poet and Dean of St Paul's Cathedral, who addressed letters and poems to her, and preached a commemorative sermon on her death. Donne and George Herbert sheltered together from the plague at her Chelsea house in 1625, when Chelsea was still a village separate from a crowded and unhealthy London.

Herbert had an outstanding academic career at Trinity College, Cambridge, composing Latin poetry, both courtly and religious, and winning appointment as University Orator. In this office he ad-

Bemerton Church, near Salisbury, with the Rectory visible behind. Here George Herbert performed the duties of a country parson. The thirteenth-century church, humble even by village standards, contrasts with the splendour of Trinity College, Cambridge, where Herbert had been an undergraduate and a fellow, and on which he turned his back.

View of Trinity College, from David Loggan, *Cantabrigia illustrata* (Cambridge, 1690).

dressed in Latin all the leading men of the kingdom who visited the University. The post of University Orator was a step on the ladder to political office. As another apparent step on that ladder, Herbert represented for a short time the family borough of Montgomery in the House of Commons.

Some early biographers claim Herbert had aspirations to a political career, and that his ambitions were disappointed by his lack of the necessary skills and by the death of patrons, not least King James in 1625. There is no direct evidence on this point. Herbert's correspondence at Cambridge shows that he envisaged ordination and, as a Fellow of Trinity College, he would have been obliged to take holy orders had he stayed on. In the event, he was ordained deacon by 1626 and priest by 1630. The late age at which he was ordained, and the gap between the two ordinations, suggest some hesitation in Herbert's commitment to the priesthood, a suggestion supported by the self-questioning that appears in his poetry.

After ordination, Herbert became Rector of Bemerton, just outside the cathedral city of Salisbury, where John Jewell had presided as bishop 60-70 years earlier. Bemerton is probably the model for the village parish of *The Country Parson*. Herbert's willingness to leave Cambridge and Westminster for Bemerton suggests that he had renounced any ambitions for worldly success and even ecclesiastical preferment. The saintly devotion with which Herbert's priest practises his vocation in *The Country Parson* supports that suggestion. On the other hand, Bemerton is within walking distance of Salisbury, seat of a powerful bishop, and its parish boundaries contained Wilton House, the residence of Herbert's relations, the Earls of Pembroke, and a centre of political and social influence. Indeed, Herbert was named to the living of Bemerton through the influence of the Earl of Pembroke. By going to Bemerton, therefore, Herbert was not necessarily exiling himself. Had he lived longer, his social rank, his abilities, and his situation under the eye of the Bishop of Salisbury would all have put him in a position to gain preferment in the church, like his friend or acquaintance Donne.

Whether such an opportunity would have presented itself, and how Herbert might have responded, we do not know. He suffered from recurrent illness, probably tuberculosis, from his Cambridge years, and he was terminally ill by 1632. He died in 1633, after only three years at Bemerton, and still a month short of his fortieth birthday.

Herbert's Poetry of the Church

Herbert's poetic contribution to the seventeenth-century formation of Anglican identity and spirituality is many-sided. His poems on the church and its priesthood form a bridge from the doctrines of the church considered in earlier chapters to the spirituality of *The Country Parson*, and to similar spiritual treasures in the writings of Jeremy Taylor and William Law in the succeeding chapters. In Herbert's poems on the church is played out also the personal drama that brings Herbert to vivid life and endears him to his readers.

In "The British Church" Herbert gives poetic form to Hooker's claim that their church represents a mean between the excesses of unreformed Catholicism on the one side and ultra-reformed Protestantism on the other. The Church of England, our "dear mother," dresses in perfectly judged taste:

> A fine aspect in fit array,
> Neither too mean, nor yet too gay,
> > Shows who is best:
> Outlandish looks may not compare;
> For all they either painted are,
> > Or else undrest.

Of those outlandish or foreign extremes, the painted one is "She on the hills" of Rome, who "wantonly allureth." At the other extreme is John Calvin's Geneva, seated below the Alps:

> She in the valley is so shy
> Of dressing, that her hair doth lie
> > About her ears

—that is, in an unladylike, slatternly fashion.

The equilibrium maintained by the English church is a rare quality, because the church in general has suffered a decline since its foundation at Pentecost or Whitsunday. In his poem on that feast, Herbert complains that the fire of the Holy Spirit lies extinguished or, at any rate, invisible; the generous hospitality of this "house of prayer for all people" has become meagre:

> Where is that fire which once descended
> On thy apostles? thou didst then
> Keep open house, richly attended,
> Feasting all comers by twelve chosen men.

The degeneration of the church largely results from the way it has torn itself apart through its internal disputes. In "Church-rents and Schisms,"[1] an intricate series of metaphors traces the fading of the bloom that is Herbert's symbol for the church. The rose is traditionally a symbol for the Virgin Mary but, since both the Virgin and the church act as mother to the Christian soul, the symbol transfers readily. Noble but delicate, prolific and finely scented, the rose is a symbol well suited to Herbert's loving ideal of the church.

> Why doth my Mother blush? is she the rose,
> And shows it so? Indeed Christ's precious blood
> Gave you a colour once; which when your foes
> Thought to let out, the bleeding did you good,
> And made you look much fresher than before.

Blushing at her deterioration, our mother the church resembles a red rose. Originally she took this colour from her participation in Christ's blood, and when her enemies caused her to bleed in acts of martyrdom, she actually gained in strength. Herbert is both remembering the aphorism that "the blood of the martyrs is the seed of the church" in its early days, and thinking of the use of controlled bleeding as a medical treatment in his own time. But the disputes of the Reformation period have had the effect of worms or insects gnawing into the flower:

> But when debates and fretting jealousies
> Did worm and work within you more and more,

> Your colour faded, and calamities
> > Turned your ruddy into pale and bleak:
> > Your health and beauty both began to break.

"Fretting" means devouring (an obsolete sense); it means leaving a filigree or network (as some insects leave after they have devoured); it means vexed or querulous (the word's modern sense). Hence the rose has lost its colour, strength, and beauty—the external attractions, stripped away by the Reformation and the Puritan movement, that draw her children to her.

However painful and lamentable the sufferings of the church, it can still fulfil its function of preaching the gospel and administering the sacraments through the agency of its priests. Priesthood is a high but difficult calling. As we will learn in *The Country Parson*, the priest must live out the gospel, teaching by example. Teaching verbally, through words alone, does not suffice. In himself as fragile as a piece of glass, the priest may yet be transformed by God's grace into a window through which the light of the gospel may shine:

> But when thou dost anneal in glass thy story,
> > Making thy life to shine within
> The holy preachers; then the light and glory
> > More reverend grows, and more doth win,
> > Which else shows wat'rish, bleak, and thin.
>
> > > > ("The Windows")

The priest who practises what he preaches is like a window shining with the life that God offers, and that was manifested in the life of Jesus, the gospel story. When this form of communication takes place, the priest becomes reverend, revered, in fact as well as in title, and wins more souls for God. If he does not live up to this ideal, he will transmit not divine light but the uninspiring "wat'rish, bleak, and thin" light of a wintry English day. The life and the teaching of the priest work on his hearers in the same way as the colours and light of stained glass work on viewers. Both tell the gospel story, in the priest by preaching and living, in stained glass by pictures.

Developing his metaphor further, Herbert draws a parallel between the window of the godly preacher and the stained glass windows of English churches:

> Doctrine and life, colours and light, in one
> > When they combine and mingle, bring
> A strong regard and awe.

The parallel shows that Herbert had a high regard for the surviving stained glass windows in English churches. This was a disputed opinion, and is an instance of Herbert's allegiance to Catholic Anglicanism, in opposition to the Puritans. Many church windows had been destroyed in the sixteenth-century Reformation and more would be destroyed not long after Herbert's death, as the Puritan movement gained ascendance politically. That period saw the Archbishop of Canterbury, William Laud, tried by Parliament in 1641-45, when his installation of stained glass windows was cited as evidence of his popish and therefore treasonous sympathies.

The key point for Herbert is not the mere existence of church windows but what he makes them symbolize: the need to embody Christian teaching, to combine "doctrine and life." Unlike the light that streams through a window, the light transmitted by merely spoken teaching fades rapidly and its lessons do not go deep:

> speech alone
> Doth vanish like a flaring thing,
> And in the ear, not conscience ring.

In the Catholic understanding, God communicates himself through both Word and Sacraments. "The H[oly] Communion" describes that sacrament as another version of the inward experience of God. As, in preaching, divine life shines "within / The holy preachers," so in the sacrament Christ does not come to us in the external form of riches, but as inner nourishment, which alone can transform our inner sinfulness:

> Not in rich furniture, or fine array,
> > Nor in a wedge of gold,

> Thou, who from me wast sold,
> To me dost now thy self convey;
> For so thou should'st without me still have been,
> Leaving within me sin:
>
> But by the way of nourishment and strength
> Thou creep'st into my breast.

The merest taste of this nourishment, all that is vouchsafed in the act of Holy Communion, has the power to distribute its forces throughout the body like a protecting army, "Meeting sin's force and art," and able to "Affright both sin and shame." This defence is inherent in the physical reality of the elements consumed in Communion, because "the Body and Blood of Christ . . . are verily and indeed taken and received by the faithful in the Lord's Supper," as was taught by the Anglican Catechism and by Hooker.

There is another layer to the operation of Holy Communion: as well as the fortification supplied by the elements of bread and wine, there is the "grace which with these elements comes." Circumventing the battle against the rebel forces of the flesh, grace arrives like a messenger who can slip through enemy lines and deliver his dispatches to the besieged soul within:

> Only thy grace, which with these elements comes,
> Knoweth the ready way,
> And hath the privy key,
> Op'ning the soul's most subtle rooms;
> While those to spirits refin'd, at door attend
> Dispatches from their friend.

Here, too, the work is done by God, who knows the way, possesses the secret key, and can open the rooms of the soul. The faithful are required to do no more than await God's relief. In one of Herbert's characteristic endings, disarmingly simple in expression but resonant in feeling and religious meaning, the soul is transformed into the inhabitants of the besieged castle of the body, who wait for the military dispatches from their friend. "Friend" means a military ally in the siege, but also the almighty and transcendent God who is yet willing to say, "Henceforth I call you not servants . . . but I have called you friends" (John 15:15).[2]

Everything taught in these poems means that the priest who preaches the Word and administers the sacraments occupies a position of high dignity and grave responsibility. Of this Herbert has no doubt: he gives it fullest expression at the opening of *The Country Parson*. What he does doubt is his own fitness to aspire to this vocation. "The Priesthood" expresses both his faith and his uncertainties. The uncertainties arise from both spiritual and physical causes, from unworthiness and from illness. Mindful of the power of the priest to bind and loose, Herbert desires to put aside the "lay-sword" which he wore as a man of high birth for the sword of God's word:

> Blest Order, which in power dost so excel,
> That with th' one hand thou liftest to the sky,
> And with the other throwest down to hell
> In thy just censures; fain would I draw nigh,
> Fain put thee on, exchanging my lay-sword
>   For that of th' holy Word.[3]

No sooner does this aspiration arise than it gives way to a sense of unfitness:

> But thou art fire, sacred and hallow'd fire;
> And I but earth and clay: should I presume
> To wear thy habit, the severe attire
> My slender compositions might consume.
> I am both foul and brittle; much unfit
>   To deal in holy Writ.

In envisaging priesthood as fire, Herbert is again remembering the descent of the Holy Spirit in tongues of flame at Pentecost. But he dreads that it may be a fire too fierce for him to endure. The garb of a priest might become a shirt of Nessus, whose poison burnt the body of Hercules when he dressed himself in it. Herbert feels both moral foulness and physical frailty. Slender and brittle in his tubercular condition, he is no Hercules.

In a prolonged back-and-forth through the following stanzas, Herbert comes to a further recognition, that God's fire might operate not destructively but like a potter's kiln, transforming earthly clay into gleaming ceramics. But fine tableware, and the great people who eat from it, and the food itself, all remain merely earthly. The priest serves up a banquet far more opulent: the holy meal of the Eucharist, "When God vouchsafeth to become our fare [food]." This realization brings Herbert back to his unworthiness for the role:

> Wherefore I dare not, I, put forth my hand
> To hold the ark, although it seems to shake
> Through th' old sins and new doctrines of our land.

In the Old Testament, Uzzah reached out to steady the ark of the covenant as it tottered on its carriage. God punished his sacrilege by instant death, despite Uzzah's good intention (2 Samuel 6:6-7). Herbert wishes to steady the church as it totters under the impact of entrenched sinfulness and the new doctrines of seventeenth-century religious controversy. But he fears that he will merit the punishment of Uzzah. As a final stage, he resolves to wait meekly until the moment when God may wish to demonstrate his power by transforming Herbert's "mean stuff" into a worthy priest.

A similar back-and-forth between the greatness of the priest's role and the unworthiness of the man who fulfils that role is worked out in "Aaron," but to very different effect. In "The Priesthood," the dangers of presumption and inadequacy prevail; in "Aaron" all is confidence, or rather faith. The wait that concludes "The Priesthood" is over; the grace of God will indeed transform the unworthy material of his priest.

The five stanzas of "Aaron" all use the same five rhyme words in the same order at the end of their five lines. The square solidity of the 5 x 5 form, and the repetition of the rhyme words, give the poem a steadfast assurance. It begins by describing the true priest, garbed in the robes of Aaron, the Old Testament type or model of the Christian priest. In the Christian context, Aaron's robes as described in Exodus

28 (mitre, breastplate, bells attached to the bottom hem) acquire a spiritual meaning:

> Holiness on the head,
> Light and perfections on the breast,
> Harmonious bells below, raising the dead
> To lead them unto life and rest:
> Thus are true Aarons dressed.

Herbert is now a priest, but he still falls far short of these spiritual qualities; indeed, he is the opposite of all that the priest should be:

> Profaneness in my head,
> Defects and darkness in my breast,
> A noise of passions ringing me for dead
> Unto a place where is no rest:
> Poor priest, thus am I dressed.

The bells do not now harmoniously ring in the resurrection; they have instead turned into noisy passions that serve as a passing bell to mark the passage of the spiritually dead Herbert to hell. The priest's garb proclaims Herbert's condemnation, another version of the shirt of Nessus.

But that is not the end of the story, thanks to Christ's ability to transform the "mean stuff" of Herbert's fallen humanity into a new man. Herbert's faith now gives him the assurance that the old Adam is dead in him and that he may assume the lineaments of the new Adam, Christ:

> Christ is my only head,
> My alone-only heart and breast,
> My only music, striking me ev'n dead,
> That to the old man I may rest,
> And be in him new-dressed.

This assurance sounds in the poem's final line, where Herbert can at last pronounce himself a priest. He does so, characteristically, with a simplicity that radiates certainty:

> Come people; Aaron's dressed.

The Country Parson

Herbert's brief treatise on the duties of the parish priest has a double title: *A Priest to the Temple, or, The Country Parson, His Character and Rule of Holy Life*. The first title was probably added by the publisher when the book appeared posthumously in 1652, aiming to take advantage of the reputation of the collection of Herbert's poetry, which was named *The Temple*. That book had first appeared, also posthumously, in 1633 and had been reprinted at least three times by 1652. *The Country Parson* was more likely Herbert's own title; certainly the book uses the term, "parson", more often than "priest." Even so, Herbert carries into this book the high and demanding idea of the priesthood expressed in his poetry.

In the preface, Herbert writes that "the way to please [God], is to feed my flock diligently and faithfully, since our Saviour hath made that the argument of a pastor's love."[4] He is referring to the beautiful episode near the end of St John's Gospel, when Christ asks three times, "Simon, son of Jonas, lovest thou me?," and "He saith unto him, Yea, Lord; thou knowest that I love thee. He saith unto him, Feed my sheep." Herbert's understanding of this text draws a direct connection between loving Christ and feeding his sheep, or performing the work of a pastor (in Latin, a shepherd). Herbert sees his role of priest to be the same as the role of an apostle and, indeed, of Peter himself.

It is typical of Herbert to set next to this Biblical statement of his mission a homely and idiomatic statement of why he has written his book. Taking his image from the sport of archery, Herbert explains that the book is written in order "that I may have a mark to aim at: which also I will set as high as I can, since he shoots higher that threatens the moon, than he that aims at a tree." The ideal of the pastor set out in the *The Country Parson* is something for Herbert to aim at; even when he falls short, he will have shot higher than if he is satisfied to aim low.

Herbert's high idea of the priesthood also appears when he traces what he calls "the direct steps of pastoral duty and authority," that is, the role of the priest in the system of redemption. Herbert traces in this way the steps that have led to the institution of a priesthood:

For first, man fell from God by disobedience. Secondly,

Christ is the glorious instrument of God for the revoking [calling back] of man. Thirdly, Christ being not to continue on earth, but after he had fulfilled the work of reconciliation, to be received up into heaven, he constituted deputies in his place, and these are priests.

Herbert is thus very clear that priesthood was instituted directly by Christ. His phraseology is similar to the language in which the Tractarians would later assert the doctrine of the apostolic succession.[5] This divine origin gives the priest dignity but also imposes duty: "The dignity, in that a priest may do that which Christ did, and by his authority, and as his vicegerent [delegate]. The duty, in that a priest is to do that which Christ did, and after his manner, both for doctrine and life." The priest earns the dignity only if he fulfils the duty; the requirement that all Christians, but especially priests, should imitate Christ (or attempt to imitate Christ) is a theme all the way through Herbert's book. It will also be a theme of the following writers in the present book, Jeremy Taylor and William Law.

Most striking about Herbert's ideal parson is how fully he enters into the life of his country parishioners. He is not a remote figure engaged in ecclesiastical affairs or Greek scholarship, but one who understands and participates in the day-to-day life of his people. "He condescends even to the knowledge of tillage, and pastorage, and makes great use of them in teaching, because people by what they understand are best led to what they understand not." Charity especially enters into this close association with the parson's people: "at hard times, and dearths, he even parts his living and life among them, giving some corn outright, and selling other at under rates; and when his own stock serves not, working those that are able to the same charity." The ability to give charity here arises because Herbert's parson has his own stock of grain. He would derive this perhaps from tithes in kind, perhaps from farming his own glebe. This is a reminder that the parson of the seventeenth century did perforce share his livelihood with his farming parishioners; almost everyone was engaged to some extent in the production of food.

While Herbert assumes that his parson will have the rank of gentleman, as was often the case in the seventeenth-century church, he also teaches him to engage with the reality of rural life at the lowest social level. Herbert draws a number of lessons from this exposure to the life of the poor:

> neither disdaineth he to enter into the poorest cottage, though he even creep into it, and though it smell never so loathsomely. For both God is there also, and those for whom God died: and so much the rather doth he so, as his access to the poor is more comfortable than to the rich [i.e., he brings the poor more comfort or support]; and in regard of himself, it is more humiliation.

(When Herbert writes of "creeping" into a cottage, he is referring to the low door and roof of the poorest dwellings.)

In his everyday tenor of living, the parson must be mindful of the ways of country society. Because "country people live hardly, and therefore as feeling their own sweat, and consequently knowing the price of money," therefore the country parson is careful not to be or to seem in any way covetous, or to do anything that will increase the people's costs. Because

> Country people . . . do much esteem their word, it being the life of buying, and selling, and dealing in the world; therefore the parson is very strict in keeping his word . . . neither will they believe him in the pulpit, whom they cannot trust in his conversation. . . . The parson's yea is yea, and nay nay.

Here, too, Herbert draws on another scriptural precept: "let your communication be, Yea, yea; Nay, nay: for whatsoever is more than these cometh of evil" (Matthew 5:37).

Living in a country parish is an education in itself. Herbert, the Cambridge don, observes that the actual lives of people instruct the parson about human nature as books cannot. Not that it is always an idyllic or innocent life—Herbert has too keen an awareness of human frailty to suppose that:

> if a man hath wherewithal to buy a spade, and yet he chooseth rather to use his neighbour's, and wear out

> that, he is covetous. . . . Country people are full of these petty injustices, being cunning to make use of another, and spare themselves: and scholars ought to be diligent in the observation of these, . . . which while they dwell in their books, they will never find; but being seated in the country, and doing their duty faithfully, they will soon discover: especially if they carry their eyes ever open, and fix them on their charge, and not on their preferment.

Herbert's last, sharp point is that parsons must do their job for its own sake, without any ambitions for advancement in the church, a point that perhaps reveals his own intentions.

Country life educates the parson in the different varieties of people, and Herbert shows how the parson must learn to adjust his manner to different situations. When he visits his parishioners,

> Those that the parson finds idle or ill employed he chides not at first, for that were neither civil nor profitable, but always in the close, before he departs from them. Yet in this he distinguisheth; for if he be a plain countryman, he reproves him plainly, for they are not sensible of fineness [not responsive to delicate language]: if they be of higher quality, they commonly are quick and sensible and very tender of reproof, and therefore he lays his discourse so, that he comes to the point very leisurely, and oftentimes, as Nathan did, in the person of another, making them to reprove themselves.

The Biblical model this time is when the prophet Nathan uses a story or parable to induce David to condemn himself for stealing the wife of Uriah (2 Samuel 12). The pervasiveness of scriptural references in *The Country Parson* is a quiet way of reminding the reader that the Bible gives guidance for every occasion in life. Studying the Bible, studying human nature, and performing the duties of a parson are three activities that continually sustain one another.

Herbert's instruction is based in a knowledge of the conduct and values of country communities that is clear-sighted and unsentimental but also charitable. There is nothing quaint about Herbert's emphasis on country life: the vast majority of the population lived in rural communities. The equivalent task for Herbert's parson today would be to adjust to life, values, and manners in an outer-suburban parish. Herbert is writing for the new breed of university-educated clergy, who must adjust their social background and training to the needs of people of lower social classes.

In developing the detail of the parson's religious attributes and pastoral priorities, Herbert stresses studying the Bible, studying theology, and preaching. For knowledge and understanding of the Bible, the first qualification is not the learning that comes from commentators. It is, instead, "a holy life, remembering what his Master saith, that 'if any do God's will, he shall know of the doctrine' " (citing John 7:17). In other words, right teaching depends on right living. There is a link between this approach to the Bible and the parson's general approach to his people, through direct personal knowledge. If he must try to make peace among his people, the parson will not preach to them but eat with them—or, rather, his eating will be a form of preaching: "sometimes, where he knows there hath been or is a little difference, he takes one of the parties and goes with him to the other, and all dine or sup together. There is much preaching in this friendliness."

When his preaching does take the form of sermons, the preacher must show his own earnestness or commitment, "by dipping and seasoning all our words and sentences in our hearts, before they come into our mouths, . . . so that the auditors may plainly perceive that every word is heart-deep." He must have a sense of his audience, "with particularizing of his speech now to the younger sort, then to the elder, now to the poor, and now to the rich. 'This is for you', and 'This is for you.' " He must use stories, which win attention: "for them also men heed and remember better than exhortations, which, though earnest, yet often die with the sermon."

Even more than preaching, perhaps, Herbert values instruction based on the catechism, which was printed in the Book of Common Prayer. For Herbert, catechizing was preferable to preaching because it was a way of teaching doctrine more directly or more personally or more interactively. In the seventeenth century, preaching was more of an exercise in learning than it is today. A sermon was usually a lengthy discourse that required a high level of comprehension, in which the hearers must proceed at the level of the speaker. In catechizing, the teacher proceeds at the level and speed of the learner, and this is salutary for the parson himself: "whereas in sermons there is a kind of state [dignity], in catechizing there is an humbleness." By sharing in his people's growing understanding of the faith, the parson therefore finds himself spiritually "growing with the growth of his parish." Catechizing is more beneficial for the student as well, because "at sermons and prayers, men may sleep or wander; but when one is asked a question, he must discover what he is"—that is, show his own understanding and character.

Therefore, when teaching the catechism, the parson leads people to put their knowledge and understanding in their own words, by questioning them,

> as thus, in the Creed: How came this world to be as it is? Was it made, or came it by chance? Who made it? Did you see God make it? Then are there some things to be believed that are not seen? Is this the nature of belief? Is not Christianity full of such things, as are not to be seen, but believed?

Herbert compares this method to the question and answer method of Socrates: "To this purpose, some dialogues in Plato were worth the reading, where the singular dexterity of Socrates in this kind may be observed, and imitated." This is one of the few places in the *The Country Parson* where Herbert's university learning is directly in evidence, and even here he introduces it as no more than a useful adjunct to the business of Christian teaching.[6]

The parson must be especially attuned to those virtues and vices which are the most subtle; he must recognize the boundary at which an action that is natural and good may cross over into one that is excessive and sinful. Vices may grow out of, and exaggerate to a pernicious degree, qualities that may begin as virtues. Those are the vices "whose natures are most stealing [i.e., steal upon one unawares], and beginnings uncertain." Herbert gives penetrating examples of the growth of greed and avarice:

> A man may be both covetous and intemperate, and yet hear sermons against both, and himself condemn both in good earnest: and the reason hereof is, ... the beginnings of them are not observed, because of the sudden passing from that which was just now lawful, to that which is presently unlawful, even in one continued action. So a man dining, eats at first lawfully; but proceeding on, comes to do unlawfully, even before he is aware; not knowing the bounds of the action, nor when his eating begins to be unlawful. So a man storing up money for his necessary provisions, both in present for his family and in future for his children, hardly perceives when his storing becomes unlawful: yet is there a period for his storing, and a point or centre, when his storing, which was even now good, passeth from good to bad.

It is the parson's difficult task to discern when legitimate needs give way to greed or avarice. Herbert's analysis of this process will have its counterpart in a similar passage by William Law (pp. 99-100).

Herbert naturally includes among the duties of the parson his conduct of the liturgy, especially the Eucharist, but this part of his duty receives less emphasis than preaching. Herbert gives most emphasis to the sacraments when he writes about ministering to those who are sick in body or soul. At this point he instructs the parson to give a beautiful eulogy of the Eucharist: "the participation of the holy sacrament, how comfortable and sovereign [effective] a medicine it is to all sin-sick souls; what strength and joy and peace it administers against all temptations, even to death itself, he plainly and generally intimateth to the disaffected or sick person, that so the hunger and thirst after it may come rather from themselves than from his persuasion."

Herbert shows sympathy with Catholic practices that were being encouraged or mandated by William Laud as Bishop of London during the years of Herbert's priesthood. Herbert regards it as the parson's duty not only to keep the church building well maintained in general, but also "at great festivals strawed, and stuck with boughs, and perfumed with incense." He wishes to revive the custom of blessing: "In the time of popery, the priest's *Benedicite* and his holy water were over-highly valued, and now we are fallen to the clean contrary, even from superstition to coldness and atheism." In these examples, Herbert associates himself with traditional churchmanship, and against the Puritans who sought to root out these Catholic continuities.

Endnotes

1 In this title "rent" has the sense of something torn. "Schism" is likewise derived from the Greek for something cut or divided.

2 Herbert's besieged castle draws on an allegory for attacks on the body or soul that has a long history in Christian poetry, originating with Prudentius in the fourth century. Two examples in English are the medieval play, *The Castle of Perseverance* (1405-25), and the episode of the Castle of Alma in Edmund Spenser's *Faerie Queene*, Book II, Canto ix (1590).

3 "And take . . . the sword of the Spirit, which is the word of God," Ephesians 6:17.

4 "Argument" is here used in its archaic meaning of "token" or "evidence."

5 See pp. 118-9, 127-9.

6 More typically, Herbert points out the insufficiency of classical learning for Christian teaching. The preacher, for example, must show "A Character, that *Hermogenes* never dreamed of, and therefore he could give no precepts thereof". Hermogenes of Tarsus wrote instructions for public speakers in the second century AD.

Further Reading

Joseph H. Summers, *George Herbert: his religion and art*. Cambridge, Mass.: Harvard University Press, 1954.

Elizabeth Clarke, *Theory and Theology in George Herbert's Poetry: "Divinitie, and Poesie, Met."* Oxford: Oxford University Press, 1997.

Philip Sheldrake, *Heaven in Ordinary: George Herbert and his writings*. Norwich: Canterbury Press, 2009.

John Drury, *Music at Midnight: the life and poetry of George Herbert*. London: Allen Lane, 2013.

Mark Oakley, *My Sour-Sweet Days: George Herbert and the journey of the soul*. London: SPCK, 2019.

The Church of St Peter and St Paul, Uppingham, Rutland, where Jeremy Taylor was Rector from 1638 to 1642, after which he was ejected by Puritan authorities. This view shows the largely fourteenth-century nave, tower, and spire that would have been known to Taylor.

6

Jeremy Taylor

Jeremy Taylor (1613-1667) was born and educated in Cambridge. His abilities were early recognized by Archbishop William Laud, and he became a chaplain to King Charles I. On the outbreak of civil war, he became a chaplain in the Royalist army. After a Royalist military defeat in Wales in 1645, Taylor was captured and imprisoned. Upon release, he kept a low profile in Wales for thirteen years as chaplain to a noble family. During this period, the 1650s, the Commonwealth, which had replaced the monarchy and was the political expression of Puritanism, abolished Anglicanism as the state religion. It was then that Taylor wrote controversial works and the devotional books for which he is most remembered.

Taylor continued to meet harassment for maintaining his Anglican faith and practices, spending more time in prison. He was financially insecure, like many of the Anglican clergy who had been deprived of their livings. Nevertheless, he did make visits to London, where he was able to preach in private houses and, on occasion, even in churches. Indeed, in 1658, still under Commonwealth rule, Taylor was appointed lecturer or preacher at Lisburn in northern Ireland, under the patronage of another nobleman. The church in Lisburn was controlled by Independents, the sect of most English Puritans, but there remained in the district a strong group of Presbyterians, who were royalists, and a group of episcopalian churchmen. These groups no longer controlled parishes but they retained an existence and an identity. There was also a majority of Roman Catholics, who cared nothing for these parties and their differences.

Taylor's career during these years witnesses to the fact that religious life under the Commonwealth had many cross-currents. The Puritan régime never succeeded in completely suppressing other forms of churchmanship: England was not Spain or Geneva, even if the Puritans strove to turn it into Geneva. It is an example of these variable religious conditions that Oliver Cromwell himself, head of state and head of government in the Commonwealth, overruled a prohibition against Taylor's taking up his appointment in Ireland and issued him a safe-conduct.

At the Restoration of church and monarchy in 1660, Taylor was appointed Bishop of Down and Connor in Ireland, and also vice-chancellor of Trinity College, Dublin. For the remaining seven years of his life he cultivated Irish education and worked energetically, not to say combatively, albeit with increasing pessimism, to build up the Church of Ireland along Anglican lines.

It was through his writings that Taylor earned the title, "teacher of the faith", which is how he is described in the Church of England calendar. In the seventeenth century, a prodigious amount of intellectual energy and numberless books, now unread except by historians, were devoted to religious controversy. In Taylor's England, this still meant especially the controversy between the Church of England and its Puritan reformers that had raged for the fifty years leading up to the Civil War.

Hooker had first framed the Anglican response to the Puritans. Taylor made his own contributions to these debates in a series of short books. *The Sacred Order and Offices of Episcopacy* was a defence of the institution of bishops, which the Puritans rejected. *On the Reverence due to the Altar* was a defence of that item of church furniture, which made its reappearance in English churches in the seventeenth century, having been for a time replaced by a plain table in the chancel. The revival of the altar was a particular project of Taylor's patron, Archbishop Laud. After the Book of Common Prayer was abolished, Taylor replied with *A Defence of Authorised and Set Forms of Liturgy*. These books all appeared in the 1640s, before or during the Civil War. In later books, Taylor would also argue the case of Anglicanism in the other direction, against the claims of Roman Catholicism. This, too, was a long-lasting area of the debate. On Eucharistic doctrine, a key area of debate, Taylor in 1654 defended the Anglican doctrine of the real presence against the Roman doctrine of transubstantiation. In 1664, when he was a bishop in Ireland, Taylor wrote *A Dissuasive from Popery: To the People of Ireland*, on behalf of all the bishops of the Church of Ireland, an attempt to persuade the mass of people who obstinately refused to succumb to the appeal of that church.

In general, Taylor certainly argues his case vigorously, but his writings are more objective and measured in their arguments and more moderate in their language than most religious controversy of the time. The same moderation appears in another of Taylor's controversial writings from the Civil War period, *The Liberty of Prophesying* (1646). This is an argument in support of a religious freedom that is more extensive than was generally allowed by any parties in the seventeenth century. "Prophesying" was a favourite word among English Puritans in the sixteenth and seventeenth centuries, when it meant publicly interpreting or expounding the Bible or Christian doctrine. The word derives from St Paul in 1 Corinthians 14. Gatherings of Puritan clergy for prophesyings, outside of church services, had been prohibited under Queen Elizabeth I. Now Taylor argues that these and other forms of religious speech should be permitted by church and state.

His premise is that justice should punish only actions, not ideas or thoughts, with the qualification that it may punish public expression of ideas or thoughts that will cause harm or disturb society. That position is close to the practice of liberal democracies. For us, it is legal to speak in support of Islamic fundamentalism or against abortion; it is not legal to incite violence against non-Moslems or urge the fire-bombing of abortion clinics. In support of this position, Taylor's reasoning is that "Force in matters of opinion can do no good, but is very apt to do hurt; for no man can change his opinion when he will . . . to use force may make him an hypocrite but never to be a right believer." In short, it is not possible to legislate ideas or belief; therefore the state must tolerate differing religious beliefs. In Taylor's lucid and humane words:

> the question, whether the prince may tolerate divers persuasions, is no more than whether he may lawfully persecute any man for not being of his opinion. . . . To believe so, or not so, when there is no more but mere believing, is not in his power to enjoin, therefore not to punish. And it is not only lawful to tolerate disagreeing persuasions, but the authority of God only is competent to take notice of it, and infallible to determine it, and fit to judge.[1]

Tolerance of the Church of Rome was a test case in this period, especially after 1570, when Pope Pius V had claimed to free the subjects of Queen Elizabeth from their allegiance, on the grounds of her heresy. Taylor's approach to this question derives from his principle that the tolerance accorded to belief does not extend to incitements to demolish political and social order:

> such doctrines as these—the pope may . . . absolve subjects from their allegiance to their natural prince; faith is not to be kept with heretics; heretical princes may be slain by their subjects— . . . these opinions are a direct overthrow to all human society . . ., a destruction of government, and of the laws, and duty.

People preaching these doctrines should therefore be punished by law. Even in this case, it remains one thing to hold such opinions privately, another to urge them publicly: "yet if he hold his peace, no man is to persecute or punish him; for then it is mere opinion, which comes not under political cognizance . . . But . . . the preaching such doctrines cannot claim the privilege and immunity of a mere opinion."

Soundly logical, this argument also has a political message. By giving religious opinion the Puritan name of prophesyings, Taylor makes the point that the Puritans, who are now in control, should give the now persecuted people of his persuasion the freedom they had once claimed for themselves. The same logic governed the limits of Taylor's tolerance when the Church of England and the Church of Ireland regained their positions as state churches. Taylor as a bishop did not hesitate to demand that clergy must either accept its principles or lose their livings, as he himself had earlier lost his living. His principle now took the reasonable form of permitting people to hold and express contrary views, but not giving them a public platform from which to do so.

Taylor's vindication of intellectual liberty does credit to Anglicanism and its contribution to Western culture at large.[2] But Taylor is remembered and admired no less for his writings about personal religious conduct and devotion. His first major book in this field is *The Great Exemplar* (1649), which takes the life of Jesus Christ as the example for our own living. In sixteen sections, from the Annunciation to the Ascension, *The Great Exemplar* narrates the principal events in the life of Jesus, giving historical context where necessary, suggesting personal motives, and weighing up post-scriptural commentaries: in these respects, it has the marks of a pioneering scholarly biography of Jesus Christ. But Taylor is also concerned to draw out of the biographical record moral lessons, teachings for our lives, and in this respect his book has the character of a collection of sermons. Each section ends with a long and impassioned prayer, helping readers to internalize in their hearts the example set by Jesus. This meditative writing of the life of Jesus was earlier undertaken by the Franciscan friar, St Bonaventura, in the thirteenth century and by the Carthusian monk, Ludolf of Saxony, in the fourteenth. Ludolf's work was read by St Ignatius Loyola and influenced his own famous system of meditation, the *Spiritual Exercises*.

In *The Great Exemplar*, Taylor teaches a practical piety, the Christian faith as a way of life. This merging of belief and practice, faith and works, is characteristic of Anglicanism. Also characteristically Anglican, deriving from Hooker, is the high value Taylor places on human reason and natural law. Like Hooker, Taylor believes that we can arrive at most religious truths and moral principles by the light of reason. Our Lord's teaching on earth restated what all can learn from "natural religion; that is, . . . such expressions of duty as all wise men and nations used." The significance of what Jesus offers is not any new idea but a supreme example of how to carry out those duties, to God and to our neighbour. In supposing that we can model ourselves on the example of Jesus, Taylor minimizes the fallen nature of humanity and maximizes the fact that we are made in God's image. His opening prayer expresses the hope that we may through our actions restore that image in ourselves:

> Holy Jesu, since thy image is imprinted on our nature by creation, let me also express thy image by all the parts of a holy life, conforming my will and affections to thy holy precepts; submitting my understanding to the dictates and lessons of perfection; imitating thy sweetness and excellencies of society, thy devotion in prayer, thy conformity to God, thy zeal tempered with meekness, thy patience heightened with charity; that heart, and hands, and eyes, and all my faculties may grow up with the increase of God, till I come to the full measure of the stature of Christ.

Such a hope limits the dominion of original sin. Indeed, Taylor believed that sin could not be inherited, that it could exist only in our own actions. He acknowledges only an "original stain", a propensity to sin. Taylor drew criticism for this view, and it may have contributed to the only qualified approval that he received from the Oxford Movement.[3] But there are ways, possibly more important ways, in which Taylor's teaching is thoroughly Catholic, one being his discussion in *The Great Exemplar* of the Eucharist, when it arises from the episode of the Last Supper. Here Taylor states a doctrine of eucharistic sacrifice that builds convincingly on the Epistle to the Hebrews, uniting the priestly actions of Christ and his church:

> Our very holding up the Son of God, and representing him to his Father, is the doing an act of mediation and advantage to ourselves in the virtue and efficacy of the Mediator. As Christ is a priest in heaven for ever, and yet does not sacrifice himself afresh, nor yet without a sacrifice could he be a priest, but by a daily ministration and intercession represents his sacrifice to God, and offers himself as sacrificed; so he does upon earth by the ministry of his servants; he is offered to God; that is, he is by prayers and the sacraments represented or offered up to God as sacrificed.

Taylor also writes eloquently on the blessings and benefits of communion, in a style that shows an intense devotion to the sacraments. Marshalling all his rhetorical techniques and imaginative metaphors, he enumerates the benefits of communion as "the relief of our sorrows, the antidote and preservative of souls, the viand [food] of our journey, the guard and passport of our death, the wine of angels." Demonstrating the breadth of his learning, he compares our eucharistic food with Renaissance medicines and with other marvellous foods from different cultures and from the Bible. He ends his catalogue by recognizing that marvels and learning are only shadows of the simple but supreme gift of Our Lord:

> it is more healthful than rhubarb, more pleasant than cassia; . . . the beetle [betel nut] and lareca of the Indians, the moly or nepenthe of Pliny, the lirinon of the Persians, the balsam of Judaea, the manna of Israel, the honey of Jonathan, are but weak expressions to tell us that . . . nothing is good enough in philosophy to become its emblem. All these must needs fall very short of those plain words of Christ, "This is my body."

Taylor's reverence for the Eucharist makes him stress the need for careful preparation, and especially repentance, before approaching communion. He encourages daily communion for the clergy and weekly communion at least for laity. These were practices little known in his time, and another example of his Catholic Anglicanism. Taylor even suggests that the decline of the Eucharist, and what the Eucharist represents, was a cause of the Civil War. His description of the moral malaise that marked Civil-War England applies just as well to our own times:

> if we consider this sacrament is intended to unite the spirits and affections of the world, . . . ("for we are one body," saith St. Paul, "because we partake of one bread,") possibly we may have reason to say, that the wars of kingdoms, the animosity of families, the infinite multitude of lawsuits, the personal hatreds, and the universal want of charity, which hath made the world miserable

and wicked, may in a great degree be attributed to the neglect of this great symbol and instrument of charity.

The Great Exemplar was probably written early in Taylor's exile in Wales. His greatest writings, from the early 1650s, are a response to that situation, when he found himself unable to pursue publicly his vocation as an Anglican priest. *Holy Living* (1650) is a guide for people faithful to Anglican tradition at a time when the church as an institution no longer existed. The teachings about conduct in this book are those that Taylor might have given from the pulpit that he no longer occupied; its prayers benefit readers who can no longer join in the daily and weekly services of the church.

But if that is the origin of the book, the way it is presented makes it more than just a substitute. *Holy Living* greatly expands the laconic concision that often marks the Book of Common Prayer, and is therefore a devotional complement to it. Long after the crisis of the church had passed, Taylor's book served as a spiritual manual for a great variety of readers. It has appeared in at least forty different editions, and many more reprints. Its devotees have included Samuel Johnson and John Wesley in the eighteenth century and Samuel Taylor Coleridge in the nineteenth. More improbably, the truculent playwright, John Osborne, in 1982 selected *Holy Living* and its companion, *Holy Dying*, as the book he would take to a desert island.

Holy Living is structured on a verse from St Paul's epistle to Titus: "we should live soberly, righteously, and godly, in this present world." The Book of Common Prayer adopts the same three terms when, at Morning and Evening Prayer, we pray to live a "godly, righteous, and sober life." "Sober" is Taylor's key term for our individual disposition and actions, the self-control that is the foundation on which to build other virtues. "Righteous" applies to our relations to others, within families, within society, all of which Taylor calls Christian justice. "Godly" means a life based in faith, hope, and love, and includes reading the Bible, praying, penitence, keeping festivals, fasting, giving alms. As an example of the breadth of his religious understanding, alms-giving for Taylor includes all kinds of help to people in all kinds of need: "the particulars of mercy or alms cannot be narrower than men's needs are, and the old method of alms is too narrow to comprise them all." Alms-giving, which Taylor also equates with mercy, therefore includes teaching the ignorant, comforting the afflicted, reconciling enemies.

A remarkable section of *Holy Living* is "the Practice of the Presence of God." Taylor here adopts a meditative and devotional practice devised in Italy and France in the sixteenth and seventeenth centuries, including by St Ignatius Loyola. The aim is to maintain a constant awareness that God's being pervades all things, and that one is therefore personally always in the company of God, performing all one's tasks, especially the most humble tasks, entirely out of love for God. Taylor sums up the presence of God thus:

> we may imagine God to be as the air and the sea, and we all enclosed in his circle, wrapped up in the lap of his infinite nature; or as infants in the wombs of their pregnant mothers: and we can no more be removed from the presence of God than from our own being.

The homely but startling imagery in which Taylor casts us as children of a maternal God, wrapped up on his lap, or unborn in the womb, shows his affinity with Herbert and other Anglican metaphysical poets of the seventeenth century such as Donne and Vaughan.

As well as by such poetic description, Taylor expounds the presence of God with a scholastic thoroughness characteristic of seventeenth-century religious writers and preachers: there are six ways in which God is present; there are ten ways to keep ourselves in mind of this presence; there are five benefits of this exercise. Though they sound dry in outline, in detail these lists show acute psychological observation and the same imagination. One of the six ways in which God is present is this:

> God is especially present in the hearts of his people by his Holy Spirit; and indeed the hearts of holy men are temples in the truth of things, and, in type and shadow, they are heaven itself. For God reigns in the hearts of his servants; there is his kingdom. . . . God dwells in our hearts by faith and Christ by his Spirit, and the Spirit by his purities: so

> that we are also cabinets of the mysterious Trinity; and what is this short of heaven itself, but as infancy is short of manhood, and letters of words? The same state of life it is, but not the same age. It is heaven in a looking-glass, dark, but yet true.[4]

Again, two of the five benefits of living in the presence of God are these:

> It produces a confidence in God and fearlessness of our enemies, patience in trouble and hope of remedy; . . . where his rod strikes us, his staff supports us . . .
>
> we are of the same household with God; he is with us in our natural actions, to preserve us; in our recreations, to restrain us; in our public actions, to applaud or reprove us; in our private, to observe us; in our sleeps, to watch by us; in our watchings, to refresh us.

These characteristic passages express the depth of Taylor's religious understanding and experience in a language that is vivid, masterful, and inspiring. Elsewhere, *Holy Living* shows the breadth as well as the depth of his mind, when he joins and harmonises Christian teaching and classical ethics. As already observed, Taylor places a high value on the powers of human nature, including human reason, believing that essential moral principles can be arrived at independent of revelation, that they are shared by "all wise men and nations." This belief is at work in Taylor's treatment of what he calls "contentedness". The term, "contentedness", has an old-fashioned flavour that may suggest complacency to contemporary readers; more approachable modern terms would be perspective or equanimity.

> We are in the world like men playing at tables:[5] the chance is not in our power, but to play it is; and when it is fallen we must manage it as we can, and let nothing trouble us. But when we do a base action, or speak like a fool, or think wickedly—these things God hath put into our powers. But concerning those things which are wholly in the choice of another, they cannot fall un-

der our deliberation, and therefore neither are they fit for our passions. My fear may make me miserable, but it cannot prevent what another hath in his power and purpose; and prosperities can only be enjoyed by them who fear not at all to lose them, since the amazement and passion concerning the future takes off all the pleasure of the present possession. Therefore if thou hast lost thy land, do not also lose thy constancy; and if thou must die a little sooner, yet do not die impatiently. For no chance is evil to him that is content; and to a man nothing is miserable unless it be unreasonable.

All would agree that this is wise advice, albeit easier said than done. Similar teachings appear in the wisdom books of the Bible, especially Ecclesiastes, and also in the Greek and Latin philosophy of the stoics—which originated at much the same time that Ecclesiastes was written. (There may have been a direct relation between Hebrew and classical thought at that time.) Taylor is in fact quoting directly from Greek writers: the image of life as a game of dice occurs in Plato and is quoted by Plutarch in his essay, *The Tranquillity of the Soul*; the aphorism, "nothing is miserable unless it be unreasonable", is a quotation from the philosopher Epictetus. In accordance with his belief in a shared and fundamental "natural religion", and the Anglican respect for human reason and human capabilities that descends from Hooker, Taylor is willing to draw on the pool of wisdom that exists outside Judaeo-Christian tradition.

Taylor's teaching on contentedness, or equanimity, is not mere theory or mere words; it emerges from his own personal circumstances, which were testing and tragic. In the game of tables that determines the externals of our lives, Taylor had seen the dice fall unfavourably. He committed himself to the losing cause in a civil war; he saw his patrons, Archbishop Laud and King Charles I, executed; his church was abolished; it was illegal for him to exercise his vocation; he was living on the charity of a wealthy family; he had been several times arrested and jailed. He is clearly thinking of his own hardships as he seeks out the sources of "contentedness":

> I am fallen into the hands of publicans and sequestrators, and they have taken all from me: what now? let me look about me. They have left me the sun and moon, fire and water, a loving wife, and many friends to pity me, and some to relieve me, and I can still discourse; and, unless I list, they have not taken away my merry countenance, and my cheerful spirit, and a good conscience; they still have left me the providence of God, and all the promises of the gospel, and my religion, and my hopes of heaven, and my charity to them too; and still I sleep and digest, I eat and drink, I read and meditate; I can walk in my neighbour's pleasant fields, and see the variety of natural beauties, and delight in all that in which God delights—that is, in virtue and wisdom, in the whole creation, and in God himself. And he that hath so many causes of joy, and so great, is very much in love with sorrow and peevishness, who loses all these pleasures, and chooses to sit down upon his little handful of thorns.

In such a passage, and there are many like it in *Holy Living*, what might have been merely the well-worn commonplaces of ethical philosophy are given life by their direct conversational expression and their proverbial pungency.[6] One scholar has pointed out that Taylor's ability to find "contentedness" when his church seems to have disappeared gives him a special interest for us today, when the church is also under threat of disappearance, or near-disappearance, from internal failings and discord, and from external hostility or indifference.

Holy Living resembles another classic manual by a seventeenth-century bishop, the *Introduction to the Devout Life* by St Francis de Sales.[7] De Sales teaches a similar practice of the presence of God, and his book is the only contemporary devotional work from which Taylor quotes.

Another book of Taylor's, *Holy Dying*, is a companion to *Holy Living*: Manuals to assist the dying and those who attended them, including the clergy, made their appearance around 1400. They teach dying as an art, *ars moriendi*. Better regarded as a spiritual practice, the *ars moriendi* usually involves contemplation of the certainty and the reality of death and judgement, and gives remedies for discontent in sickness and for the fear of death. Taylor's contribution to this devotional genre is to teach that the art of dying, holy dying, must grow out of the art of living, holy living. Only by a good life can one prepare for a good death. Taylor gives exercises for repentance, a regular feature of the *ars moriendi*, but he disparages the idea of deathbed repentance, again because repentance is complete only when we actively change our life.

Taylor's eloquence reaches one of its most remarkable heights in *Holy Dying*, when he catalogues the multifarious ways in which we may meet death. The detail and comprehensiveness and vividness of this tremendous passage are best appreciated if it is broken up on the page. That presentation helps the reader appreciate Taylor's rhetorical devices of anaphora (or repetition), of parallelism, of antithesis, as he persuades our reluctant minds to contemplate the only certainty of life, which is death:

> Death meets us everywhere, and is procured by every instrument, and in all chances, and enters in at many doors;
>
> by violence and secret influence;
>
> by the aspect of a star and the stink of a mist; . . .
>
> by the fall of a chariot and the stumbling at a stone;
>
> by a full meal or an empty stomach;
>
> by watching [staying awake] at the wine or by watching at prayers;
>
> by the sun or the moon;
>
> by a heat or a cold;
>
> by sleepless nights or sleeping days; . . .
>
> by God's mercy or God's anger;
>
> by everything in providence and everything in manners;
>
> by everything in nature and everything in chance. . . .
>
> we take pains to heap up things useful to our life, and get our death in the purchase;

and the person is snatched away, and the goods remain.

And all this is the law and constitution of nature;

it is a punishment to our sins, the unalterable event of Providence, and the decree of Heaven.

The chains that confine us to this condition are strong as destiny, and immutable as the eternal laws of God.[8]

Endnotes

[1] A precedent for this approach was provided by Queen Elizabeth I, who is said to have declared that she did not wish to "make a window into men's souls." Her régime required outward conformity, attendance at the services of the Church of England, but did not investigate inner beliefs, a practice associated with the Inquisition of the Roman Catholic church.

[2] Two years before Taylor's *Liberty of Prophesying*, John Milton had published *Areopagitica* (1644), a shorter essay arguing against the licensing (in effect the censorship) of books. Milton's argument defends the need to examine any and all ideas in order to arrive at truth. John Locke's *Letter Concerning Toleration* (1689) is more famous in the history of philosophy than Taylor's book, but in fact repeats many of Taylor's arguments.

[3] In one of his contributions to the Tracts for the Times, John Keble argued that the church, through its bishops, needed to give more active guidance on matters of doctrine. By way of example, he writes,

> If, when the excellent Bishop Taylor published his *Liberty of Prophesying*, there had been a council of primitive bishops at hand, to warn him authoritatively of the evil consequences which heretics would afterwards draw from some of his positions, the church would, in all probability, have been a gainer in two ways: first, what he had there put incautiously would have been corrected, and the sting taken out: and next, we might so much the more unreservedly use his authority on other points. (Tract 54)

Even so, the Tracts do acknowledge Taylor's authority. Tract 71, recommending the Fathers of the Church as a guide to ascertaining true Catholic doctrine, says that "their directions are distinctly propounded and supported by our divines of the seventeenth century", among whom it specifies Taylor for his "great and concordant principles and doctrines." Taylor is quoted as an authority on fasting (Tract 18), on episcopacy (Tract 74), and on the daily recitation of the offices of Morning and Evening Prayer (Tract 84).

4 Looking-glasses or mirrors in Taylor's time, as in St Paul's time, were made of polished brass, and did not give back the bright image we receive from a glass mirror. (Hence, in 1 Corinthians 13:12, we "see through a glass darkly", that is, as if in a mirror, and therefore incompletely.)

5 "Tables" was the name for a game of chance like backgammon; the phrase, "to turn the tables," derives from that game. The rest of the sentence means that, just as we have no control in a game of chance, so we have no power in determining the course of our lives, but we do have the power to join in the game and to make the best of the way the dice falls.

6 Taylor's description of his simple contentments recalls the Tudor poet Sir Thomas Wyatt, in his satire, *Mine own John Poynz*. Wyatt fell from favour at the court of Henry VIII, and he, too, was imprisoned for a time. His satire describes the fickleness of court life and concludes with the consolations of country life (though Wyatt's pleasure in hunting identifies him as gentry, not a clergyman scholar):

> This maketh me at home to hunt and to hawk,
> And in foul weather at my book to sit;
> In frost and snow then with my bow to stalk;
> No man doth mark whereso I ride or go:
> In lusty leas at liberty I walk. . . .
> But here I am in Kent and Christendom
> Among the Muses where I read and rhyme.

7 *L'Introduction à la vie dévote* (Rouen, 1608). This book had an even wider circulation than *Holy Living*, with 40 editions in the remaining fourteen years of the author's lifetime.

8 The opening of the passage recalls another English writer, the dramatist John Webster, in *The Duchess of Malfi* (1613-14):

> I know death hath ten thousand several doors
> For men to take their exits; and 'tis found
> They go on such strange geometrical hinges,
> You may open them both ways.

Further Reading

H. Trevor Hughes, *The Piety of Jeremy Taylor*. London: Macmillan, 1960.

H. E. L. Huntley, *Jeremy Taylor and the Great Rebellion: a study of his mind and temper*. Ann Arbor: University of Michigan Press, 1970.

H. R. McAdoo, *First of Its Kind: Jeremy Taylor's life of Christ. A study in the functioning of moral theology*. Norwich: Canterbury Press, 1994.

Reginald Askew, *Muskets and Altars: Jeremy Taylor and the last of the Anglicans*. London: A. R. Mowbray, 1997.

7

William Law

William Law (1686-1761), like George Herbert and Jeremy Taylor before him, turned aside from the trodden path of ecclesiastical preferment. He began as a fellow of Emmanuel College, Cambridge, but, in 1714, when the House of Hanover succeeded the Stuarts on the throne of the United Kingdom, Law's conscience did not permit him to take the necessary oath of allegiance; he considered he would be breaking his earlier oath to the Stuarts.[1] In an earlier generation, some clergy likewise refused to take the oath of allegiance to William III and Mary II when they took the throne in place of James II, in 1688. That more numerous group were known as the Nonjurors; Law was a new-generation Nonjuror.[2] Refusal to swear allegiance to the new ruling house meant that Law could neither retain his college fellowship nor receive any preferment in the established church. A serious step to take, it is an early example of the strict logic and integrity with which Law approached all his religious duties.

Law passed his enforced retirement in two places. For fourteen years he lived in the household of the Gibbon family in Putney, then a village outside London. He was tutor to Edward Gibbon, father of the famous historian of the Roman Empire. In his autobiography, the historian, born too late to have known Law personally, describes how he was remembered as "the much-honoured friend and spiritual director" of the family. It was in the Gibbon household that Law wrote his great book, *A Serious Call to a Devout and Holy Life*. In 1740, aged 56, Law returned to the village in Northamptonshire where he was born, King's Cliffe. He lived there, in a small religious community, for the last twenty-one years of his life. His companions were Hester Gibbon, the historian's unmarried aunt, and the widowed Elizabeth Hutcheson. These two ladies had a combined annual income of more than £2,500, about $1,000,000 today, while Law himself had received substantial gifts from admirers of his writings. The group used these resources to undertake the work of educating the children and relieving the poor of their village, building schools and housing, and distributing food, money, and clothes.

In creating his community, Law makes clear that he is reviving the practice of the early church:

> Ever since the beginning of Christianity there have been two orders, or ranks of people, amongst good Christians.
>
> The one that feared and served God in the common offices and business of a secular worldly life.
>
> The other, renouncing the common business and common enjoyments of life, as riches, marriage, honours, and pleasures, devoted themselves to voluntary poverty, virginity, devotion, and retirement, that by this means they might live wholly unto God, in the daily exercise of a divine and heavenly life.

In outlining this double model, Law rejected the received view, an act of faith for English Protestants over some centuries (and enthusiastically propagated by Edward Gibbon in his history), that religious communities are repositories of superstition and idleness. On the contrary, members of religious communities "would be so far from being chargeable with any superstition, or blind devotion, that they might be justly said to restore that piety, which was the boast and glory of the church, when its greatest saints were alive." As his authority, Law cites "the famous ecclesiastical historian Eusebius, who lived . . . when the church was in its greatest glory and purity, when its bishops were so many holy fathers and eminent saints." In reviving ancient Catholic practice, and in defending it on the authority of the early Fathers, Law is anticipating the practices and the arguments of the Oxford Movement. Indeed, the leaders of the Oxford Movement include Law in the company of the Anglican Fathers who

Lime Grove, the family home of the Gibbon family, in an engraving of 1846. In these pastoral surroundings outside London, William Law resided from 1723 to 1737 as "the much-honoured friend and spiritual director" of the family, and wrote his *Serious Call to a Devout and Holy Life* (1729). The historian Edward Gibbon was born at Lime Grove in 1737.

have transmitted Catholic tradition. In Tract 74, Newman cited his defence of the doctrine of the apostolic succession. Newman here drew on Law's polemical writings, but he could equally have cited his *Serious Call*, which has a fine passage on the dignity of the "apostolical calling" of a bishop. In Tract 89, Keble, answering the Protestant warning that Catholic practice may err in making too much of religious externals or symbols, points out one may err also by building too much on Evangelical ideas: "such a caution might be occasionally needed as Wesley is reported to have received from William Law: "Remember that a man may deceive himself as easily by the phrase, 'justification by faith,' as by any other combination of syllables."

Law's early writings were in defence of his Nonjuror principles. In the Church of England, the spokesman for the Hanoverian dynasty and its Whig politics was Bishop Benjamin Hoadly. Under the impact of the Civil War and the bitter religious conflicts of the seventeenth century, the Whig party opposed the continuing Stuart tendency to absolute monarchy and aimed to attract Protestant dissenters back to the Church of England. Hoadly regarded the Nonjurors, with their Jacobite sympathies and their adoption of more Catholic rites and practices, as a danger to the Protestant character of England and its church. Hoadly asserted the right of the state to deprive bishops and others of their offices if they were a threat to the state. As a corollary to that political position, his theology minimized the status of the church and clergy. Since Jesus Christ is the "sole law-giver to his subjects, and sole judge, in matters relating to salvation," "he hath . . . left behind him, no visible, human authority; no vicegerents, who can be said properly to supply his place; no interpreters, upon whom his subjects are absolutely to depend; no judges over the consciences or religion of his people."

In treatises answering Hoadly, Law argued for the importance of the apostolic succession, which gives authority to bishops; unless Christ appointed a ministry, there are no grounds for deciding who may officiate in the church. Hoadly argued that "You cannot expect the grace of God from any hands but his own without affronting him"; Law answered that Scripture shows that "it has always been God's ordinary method to dispense his blessings and judgements by the hands of men." It was also for this doctrine of a church founded by Jesus Christ that the Oxford Movement would embrace Law as one of the Fathers of Catholic Anglicanism.[3]

Law is now remembered for his *Serious Call to a Devout and Holy Life*, published in 1729. The language of the title is discomfiting to modern ears; we are rightly reluctant to label ourselves as "holy," and the word "devout" is rarely in use today. By way of normalizing that word: *devout* is the adjective derived from the noun *devotion*; both words derive from the Latin *devotus* which, in Roman religion, signified something offered up or handed over to a god as an offering or sacrifice. More generally, in Latin—as in English—a person could be devoted or dedicated to a nation or to a calling or to another person. That is how Law explains the word "devout" in the opening lines of his book: "Devotion signifies a life given, or devoted, to God."

A life given to God: Law teaches what is involved in that devotion, or commitment (to use language more likely to be employed nowadays). Law's commitment proves to be thoroughgoing, unqualified, absolute, to a degree that is challenging, even terrifying, to our everyday selves. "He, therefore, is the devout man, who lives no longer to his own will, or the way and spirit of the world, but to the sole will of God, who considers God in everything, who serves God in everything." Law means every one of those words, which is why his call to this way of living is "serious": there can be no devotion or commitment to God that is partial or provisional. Our devotion, our commitment must be all, or it may as well be nothing.[4]

For Law, devotion is expressed through both prayer and daily living. The word "devotion" is more usually attached to our prayer life, but Law warns against supposing that prayer is enough. He defers prayer until the second half of his book; the first half shows how devotion, giving our life to God, is expressed in action. Law finds a Biblical basis for this priority:

> there is not one command in all the Gospel for public worship; and perhaps it is a duty that is least insisted upon in Scripture of any other. . . . Whereas that religion or devotion which is to govern the ordinary actions of

> our life is to be found in almost every verse of Scripture. Our blessed Saviour and his apostles are wholly taken up in doctrines that relate to common life. They call us to renounce the world, and differ in every temper and way of life, from the spirit and the way of the world.

In his emphasis on "the ordinary actions of our life" as the place where religion expresses itself, Law shows himself a product of the eighteenth century. That period witnessed a reaction against the violent doctrinal disputes of the two preceding centuries. The reaction has been observed in the attitudes of Bishop Hoadly. While Law disagreed with Hoadly on the need to preserve a church and clergy established by divine authority, he did share his emphasis on the practical expression of Christianity.

Law can argue powerfully from Biblical evidence, as in the passage just quoted, but he does not cite Biblical authority very often. He draws primarily upon "these admonitions and instructions, which we receive from our senses, from an experience of the state of human life," in other words, from reason. He does on occasion "add the lights of religion, those great truths which the Son of God has taught us." Taken together, reason and Scripture make it "as much past all doubt, that there is but one happiness for man, as that there is but one God." It is less possible to argue now than in the early eighteenth century that reason self-evidently leads to belief in God and the scriptures, so we cannot expect Law's conclusion to meet general acceptance. But within a Christian framework, however arrived at, Law's argument remains powerful, though perhaps "argument" is the wrong word; it is his moral clarity and devotional fervour that speak to us.

The basis of Law's "serious call," his habitual logic, is as follows: if any degree of devotion is good, then a complete life of devotion is better; conversely, if it is allowable to fall short in any part of our devotion or commitment, then it is allowable to abandon it totally. There are many examples of this pattern of thought in his book:

> Either this piety, and wisdom, and devotion is to go through every way of life, and to extend to the use of everything, or it is to go through no part of life. . . .

If we might forget ourselves, or forget God, if we might disregard our reason, and live by humour and fancy, in anything, or at any time, or in any place, it would be as lawful to do the same in everything, at fancy, at every time, and every place.

Likewise, if it is agreed that it is wrong to commit major sins, it must likewise be agreed that it is equally wrong to commit what are called minor sins or negligences. Nor can we be selective in forgiving: "That which is a reason for forgiving one offence, is the same reason for forgiving all offences. For such charity has nothing to recommend it to-day, but what will be the same recommendation of it to-morrow." Generosity, or charity, must be constant, not occasional:

> there is the same goodness, the same excellency, and the same necessity of being . . . charitable at one time as at another. It is as much the best use of our money, to be always doing good with it, as it is the best use of it at any particular time; so that that which is a reason for a charitable action, is as good a reason for a charitable life.

Law's emphasis on active devotion over prayerful devotion is based on the same logic:

> if this be the reason of verbal praises and thanksgivings to God, because we are to live unto God all possible ways, then it plainly follows, that we are equally obliged to worship and glorify God in all other actions that can be turned into acts of piety and obedience to him. And, as actions are of much more significance than words, it must be a much more acceptable worship of God, to glorify him in all the actions of our common life, than with any little form of words at any particular times.

The great impediment to giving ourselves fully to God may be gross sinfulness, but it can also be something less obvious—too strong an attachment to things that are not harmful in themselves but become harmful if they occupy a disproportionate place in our lives, if they get in the way of devotion. Law writes perceptively on this point:

> What is more innocent than rest and retirement? And yet what more dangerous than sloth and idleness? What is more lawful than eating and drinking? And yet what more destructive of all virtue, what more fruitful of all vice, than sensuality and indulgence?
>
> Now it is for want of religious exactness in the use of these innocent and lawful things, that religion cannot get possession of our hearts. And it is in the right and prudent management of ourselves, as to these things, that all the art of holy living chiefly consists.[5]

"The art of holy living" is a significant phrase, because an art is the exercise of a skill, so the phrase implies that we can attain holiness through our human powers. Like Hooker and Taylor before him, Law has a lofty idea of the capabilities of human nature; indeed, like Taylor, he does not appear to view it as inherently and fundamentally corrupted. In a beautifully limpid passage Law sums up our created nature and its shortcomings:

> What are our real needs?—God Almighty has sent us into the world with very few wants; meat, and drink, and clothing, are the only things necessary in life; and as these are only our present needs, so the present world is well furnished to supply these needs. . . . This is the state of man,—born with few wants, and into a large world very capable of supplying them.
>
> But, alas! though God, and nature, and reason, make human life thus free from wants and so full of happiness; yet our passions, in rebellion against God, against nature and reason, create a new world of evils and fill human life with imaginary wants, and vain disquiets.

We become discontented with our natural state because of what Law calls our passions, the patterns of attraction and repulsion that constantly make us wish for what we do not have and find discontent in what we do have. In other words, we live out the Fall of man. But that is not inevitable: we can—or we can hope to—live in contentment and in accordance with nature, reason, and religion. There is no necessity that our rebellious passions must prevail:

> So far, therefore, as you reduce your desires to such things as nature and reason require; so far as you regulate all the motions of your heart by the strict rules of religion, so far you remove yourself from that infinity of wants and vexations, which torment every heart that is left to itself.[6]

What, then, is the relation between human capability and the need for divine grace?

> This doctrine does not suppose that we have no need of divine grace, or that it is in our own power to make ourselves perfect. It only supposes, that through the want of a sincere intention of pleasing God in all our actions we fall into such irregularities of life as by the ordinary means of grace we should have power to avoid.

God's grace is always available. We must cultivate the intention and exercise the self-discipline that enable us to benefit from grace. Such is the art of holy living, according to Law.

Law issued his "serious call" in 1729. As already mentioned, eighteenth-century England experienced a change of religious mood as it emerged from the bitter conflicts of the previous century, many of which originated in theology and which ended in civil war. In the church, one change was a less emphatic preoccupation with doctrines of original sin and total depravity. This is true of the Church of England (and also of continental Lutheranism). It is less true of Calvinism, whose single-minded influence had been a factor in giving original sin and total depravity their prominence in the preceding centuries. In eighteenth-century Anglicanism, sin does not govern us with the overwhelming power accorded to it in much of the theology of the previous century. Reason now has a greater role and a greater efficacy. A confidence in reason has a long lineage in Anglican thought, but its prominence in Law must also be related to the impact of thinkers like Newton and Locke, from the generation before Law, and Voltaire, his contemporary. Law writes his *Serious Call* from within the eighteenth-century Enlightenment, and he appeals to its favoured intellectual attributes of nature and reason.

Nevertheless, reason for Law conducts us to an intense piety, a profound religious commitment. It did not lead to a tepid, easy-going religion, which was one tendency within the eighteenth-century church. Law's aim is to call the reader out of that routine religion, by showing that the reason on which it based itself demands a more fervent devotion. He has one of his logical answers to those who are not prepared to go all the way in their religious commitment, to give themselves wholly to God, who are content with a moderate measure of religion—a Sunday religion:

> Most people... suppose that the strict rules and restraints of an exalted piety are such contradictions to our nature, as must needs make our lives dull and uncomfortable.
>
> This objection supposes that religion, moderately practised, adds much to the happiness of life; but that such heights of piety as the perfection of religion requireth, have a contrary effect....
>
> It supposes, therefore, that it is happy to be kept from the excesses of envy, but unhappy to be kept from other degrees of envy. That it is happy to be delivered from a boundless ambition, but unhappy to be without a more moderate ambition. It supposes, also, that the happiness of life consists in a mixture of virtue and vice, a mixture of ambition and humility, charity and envy, heavenly affection and covetousness. All which is as absurd as to suppose that it is happy to be free from excessive pains, but unhappy to be without more moderate pains: or that the happiness of health consisted in being partly sick and partly well.

It is always a matter of all or nothing—and the "all" is what brings true happiness. Giving ourselves wholly to God, living perpetually in his presence, in the awareness of his power and goodness, that is true happiness: "how can we have the least glimpse of joy or comfort, how can we have any peaceful enjoyment of ourselves, but by living wholly unto that God, using and doing everything conformably to His will?"

Law interprets the Biblical parable of the talents as a condemnation of half-heartedness. The man given a single talent "went and digged in the earth, and hid his lord's money," he does nothing with it; when called to account he explains, "Lord, I knew thee that thou art an hard man, . . . And I was afraid, and went and hid thy talent in the earth." Law explains:

> Here you see how happy this man made himself, by not acting wholly according to his Lord's will. It was, according to his own account, a happiness of murmuring and discontent; I knew thee, says he, that thou wast an hard man: it was a happiness of fears and apprehensions; . . . it was a happiness of vain labours and fruitless travails . . . this is the happiness of all those who look upon a strict and exalted piety, that is, a right use of their talent, to be a dull and melancholy state of life.

True happiness is devotion, giving oneself totally to God; holding back arises from a mistrust of God's offer.

A feature of Law's method, and one that lends his book vitality, is his use of verbal portraits, what in literary history are called "characters," examples of social or moral types. This method may be traced back to the ancient Greek philosopher, Theophrastus; in Law's period it was revived in England by the essayists Joseph Addison and Samuel Johnson and the poets John Dryden and Alexander Pope. Law's "character" of Flatus is a man in quest of an external happiness that always eludes him:

> Every time you visit him, you find some new project in his head; . . . His sanguine temper, and strong passions, promise him so much happiness in everything, that he is always cheated, and is satisfied with nothing.

> At his first setting out in life, fine clothes were his delight, his inquiry was only after the best tailors and peruke-makers [wig-makers], and he had no thoughts of excelling in anything but dress. . . .
>
> The next thing that seized his wandering imagination was the diversions of the town: and for more than a twelvemonth you heard him talk of nothing but ladies, drawing-rooms, birthnights, plays, balls, and assemblies. But, growing sick of these, he had recourse to hard drinking. . . .
>
> for two or three years, nothing was so happy as hunting; he entered upon it with all his soul, and leaped more hedges and ditches than had ever been known in so short a time. . . . No sooner had Flatus outdone all the world in the breed and education of his dogs, built new kennels, new stables, and bought a new hunting-seat, but he . . . gave away the dogs, and was, for some time after, deep in the pleasures of building.
>
> The next year he leaves his house unfinished, . . . [and] the happiest thing he could think of next, was to go abroad and visit foreign countries; . . . The next month he returned home, unable to bear any longer the impertinence of foreigners.

The name Flatus means blowing; this is the person who is blown about by his changeable desires and ideas. Flatus has a female counterpart, Feliciana. In this character Law describes the life of pleasure of an eighteenth-century gentlewoman, whose consumption of different pleasures actually becomes monotonous and wearisome, as marked in Law's style by the repetition of the word "again":

> She is to be again dressed fine, and keep her visiting day. She is again to change the colour of her clothes, again to have a new head-dress, . . . She is again to see who acts best at the playhouse, and who sings finest at the opera. She is again to make ten visits in a day, and

be ten times in a day trying to talk artfully, easily, and politely, about nothing.

She is to be again delighted with some new fashion; and again angry at the change of some old one. . . . She is to be again pleased with hypocritical compliments, and again disturbed at imaginary affronts.

Law's "characters" depict people of high social rank or, at any rate, economic privilege. His book is mostly directed to such people. This is partly because they are in a position to do most good by the use of their wealth. It is also no doubt because Law was responding to another historical change: the increase in wealth and the expansion of trade that accompanied the emergence of the British Empire in the early eighteenth century. That historical development increased the size of a moneyed and leisured class, introduced new luxuries, and turned London into a centre where new products were bought and sold and consumption was put on show on a larger scale than before. It is the society sketched in the satires of Alexander Pope at exactly the same date as Law's *Serious Call*; like Pope, Law takes a satirical attitude to what he calls "this polite age of ours," which puts social niceties before the spirit of devotion. Like Pope, Law means his satirical "characters" to function as a means of teaching:

> characters of this kind, the more folly and ridicule they have in them, provided that they be but natural, are most useful to correct our minds; and . . . [as] we best learn the nature of things, by looking at that which is contrary to them; so perhaps we best apprehend the excellency of wisdom, by contemplating the wild extravagancies of folly.

After showing how to give one's life to God through action, the second part of *A Serious Call* treats the life of prayer. Law has a system of daily prayer that is his personal adaptation of the canonical hours of monastic tradition, with six "hours" instead of eight. He is strong on the duty to rise early to pray (his equivalent to Lauds and Prime). After that, he shapes his prayer day around certain virtues, in a personal and original pattern. Prayer at 9 am (traditionally Terce) is centred on humility. Prayer at noon (Sext) is centred on universal love, manifested in prayer for others, intercession. Devotion at 3pm (Nones) is centred on resignation to the will of God. Evening prayer (Vespers) is centred on confession and repentance. Night prayer, before bed (Compline), is centred on death, and our need to "make every day a day of preparation for it."

Law takes the opportunity to offer instruction about the virtues associated with his offices of prayer, especially the morning prayer of humility, to which he gives three or four chapters. "As we are born in sin, so in pride, which is as natural to us as self-love, and continually springs from it. And this is one reason why Christianity is so often represented as a new birth, and a new spirit." We have to re-fashion our selves by unlearning the lessons of success and eminence and happiness as they are taught by "the world." To enforce this understanding, Law writes in the literary genre of the *contemptus mundi*, which occurs in Graeco-Roman, Hebrew, and Christian traditions, and which exhibits all that is unsatisfying or futile in the values of "the world":

> to lessen your fear and regard to the opinion of the world, think how soon the world will disregard you, and have no more thought or concern about you, than about the poorest animal that died in a ditch . . .
>
> Think upon the rich, the great, and the learned persons, that have made great figures, and been high in the esteem of the world; many of them died in your time, and yet they are sunk, and lost, and gone, and as much disregarded by the world, as if they had been only so many bubbles of water.

This last point is the topos of *ubi sunt*, where are they now? what has become of them? To which the implied answer is, they have turned to dust, they are as if they had never been. The term derives from the apocryphal Book of Baruch, *ubi sunt principes gentium . . .?* "Where are the princes of the heathen become, and such as ruled the beasts upon the earth; . . . and they that hoarded up silver and gold?" Law enlists these ancient forms of teaching in his call to the life of devotion.

As well as unlearning the teachings of the world, we must learn and exercise humility positively. This is done most fully by becoming the servant of the poor. Like Herbert's country parson, Law's devout person gives himself or herself over wholeheartedly to the service of the poor. The commitment Law demands is all the more striking because he is addressing himself largely to people of privilege:

> Be glad therefore to know the wants of the poorest people, and let your hands be employed in making such mean and ordinary things for them, as their necessities require....
>
> The humility also of this employment will be as beneficial to you as the charity of it. It will keep you from all vain and proud thoughts of your own state and distinction in life, and from treating the poor as creatures of a different species.... You will reverence their state and condition, think it an honour to serve them, and never be so pleased with yourself as when you are most humbly employed in their service.

This humility is also an imitation of Christ: "This will make you true disciples of your meek Lord and master, who came into the world not to be ministered unto, but to minister; and though he was Lord of all, and amongst the creatures of his own making, yet was amongst them as one that serveth."

Law's exhaustive regimen of prayer is not easily compatible with working for a living, another sign that his likely readership is a privileged class. He acknowledges this restriction, and gives good advice to people who cannot find the time for his full schedule:

> though people of leisure seem called more particularly to this study of devotion, yet persons of much business or labour must not think themselves excused ... For the greater their business is, the more need they have of some such method as this, to prevent its power over their hearts, to secure them from sinking into worldly tempers, and preserve a sense and taste of heavenly things in their minds. And a little time regularly and constantly

> employed to any one use or end, will do great things, and produce mighty effects.

That is advice that manuals of prayer and meditation have always given: a little time is better than none. Other well-tested advice that Law gives is to use a regular place and regular times for prayer. He advises the use of a crucifix for meditation, a practice that would not have been usual in eighteenth-century England. He recommends a combination of fixed prayers and personal prayers. For fixed forms of prayer, he makes the point that is always made in defence of liturgical prayer: fixed forms mean that our prayer life is not at the command of our variable feelings, sometimes eager, sometimes reluctant.

On the other hand, an admixture of personal prayer, prayer "at liberty," does allow for and adjust to those inevitable variations, "changing, improving, and suiting our devotions to the condition of our lives, and the state of our hearts." (Herbert's country parson also combines "daily prayers enjoined him by authority" with "some other . . . hours for prayers," which will keep "his soul fervent, active, young.") Every office should begin with a psalm, which we should sing: "As singing is a natural effect of joy in the heart, so it has also a natural power of rendering the heart joyful." It is not important whether or not you are a good singer: "For as it is speaking, and not graceful speaking, that is a required part of prayer; . . . so it is singing, and not artful, fine singing, that is a required way of praising God." Singing is also an example of the outward acts through which the inward worship of the heart must be expressed; both soul and body should be exercised in worship.

We may take leave of William Law with a characteristic teaching: logically consistent, Biblical, sharply challenging to our everyday assumptions. Law's community was famous for giving alms to all comers, with no questions asked. The neighbouring villagers complained that this charity attracted a flock of undeserving parasites. This is the answer of Law's character, Miranda, a female model for the devout and holy life:

> It may be . . . that I may often give to those that do not deserve it, or that will make an ill use of my alms. But

what then? Is not this the very method of Divine goodness? Does not God make "His sun to rise on the evil and on the good"? ... shall I withhold a little money, or food, from my fellow-creature, for fear he should not be good enough to receive it of me? Do I beg of God to deal with me, not according to my merit, but according to his own great goodness; and shall I be so absurd as to withhold my charity from a poor brother, because he may perhaps not deserve it? Shall I use a measure towards him, which I pray God never to use towards me?

Endnotes

[1] Law believed that the crown should pass to the Pretender, or claimant, James Stuart, who had the right of inheritance, but who, as a Roman Catholic, was excluded from the succession by the Act of Settlement of 1701. The majority of clergy who swore allegiance to the Hanoverian king considered that the Act of Settlement overrode any previous oaths. Law evidently thought otherwise, and believed that fidelity to his oath was more important than thwarting the pope.

[2] The nine nonjuring bishops were removed from office, but, otherwise, not all the first-generation Nonjurors lost their livings.

[3] In the last stage of his life, Law became an admirer and disciple of the German mystic, Jakob Böhme. Law translated Böhme and wrote a number of books explaining his mysticism. This is a side of Law that would not have met the approval of the Oxford Movement and that certainly lacks elements of Catholic orthodoxy. Böhme's "life in the new regeneration" or "angelical life," as explained by Law, does not envisage a church, scriptures, or even a historical Jesus. From vindicating the Catholic doctrine of the church against Hoadly, it seems that, under the influence of Böhme, Law came close to discarding the church. It is known, however, that Law continued to attend church, even that Hanoverian church in which he refused to officiate.

[4] As suggested earlier, the implacable logic that governs his religious thinking was also what made Law refuse to transfer his sworn allegiance from the Stuart to the Hanoverian monarchy.

[5] Compare Herbert's analysis of the way in which lawful actions shade into unlawful, or innocence into sinfulness, pp. 73-4.

⁶ Law has arrived at the same analysis of human nature as Siddartha Gautama, the Buddha, in the sixth or fifth century BC. Both analyses are based on observation and experience. The Buddhist analysis locates the source of human suffering in ignorance, attachment, and aversion. In Law's terms, these are our "rebellion against . . . reason, . . . imaginary wants, and vain disquiets." In Buddhism, an eightfold path of ethical conduct and mental discipline is designed to conduct us out of suffering. Law has an equivalent prescription in his advice to reduce one's desires and regulate the motions of one's heart.

Further Reading

Henry Broxap, *The Later Non-jurors*. Cambridge: Cambridge University Press, 1924.

Henri A. Talon, *William Law: a study in literary craftsmanship*. London: Rockliff, 1948.

John Hoyles, *The Edges of Augustanism: the aesthetics of spirituality in Thomas Ken, John Byrom and William Law*. The Hague: Martinus Nijhoff, 1972.

A. Keith Walker, *William Law: his life and thought*. London: SPCK, 1973.

8

John Keble

John Keble (1792-1866) was one of the founders of the Oxford Movement which, in the mid-nineteenth century, re-asserted and broadened the Catholic basis of Anglicanism. Keble had a brilliant career at Oxford, where he became a fellow of Oriel College, then a leading college academically and later the powerhouse of the Oxford Movement. At the age of thirty, he left Oxford for family reasons, and eventually became vicar of the country parish of Hursley, near Winchester, where he served for thirty years, until his death. Even when not resident at Oxford he kept up his connections there, contributing to the series of Tracts for the Times that spread the teachings of the Oxford Movement. He also issued translations, editions, and biographies of early church Fathers and earlier Anglican figures who embodied the ideals of the Oxford Movement.

As well as being both scholar and pastor, Keble won fame as a poet. Like Herbert, Keble has therefore left a body of writing that teaches through the pleasures of poetic language as well as more directly—in Herbert's case, his manual for a country parson, in Keble's, his sermons as one such country parson. We associate the Oxford Movement with a revived theology of the church and a revived attention to liturgy, but Keble's writings show that, at the heart of the Oxford Movement, there was also and always a deeply meditated relation to the Bible and a deep personal spirituality.

Keble's Poetry

Keble's collection, *The Christian Year*, is said to have been the most widely read poetry book of the nineteenth century. Unlike Herbert's poetry, Keble's does not arrest the reader's attention through startling language or metaphor or through imaginative leaps. He did not aim at those qualities, and his many nineteenth-century readers must not have sought them. In his Oxford lectures as Professor of Poetry, Keble lamented the late romantic poetry of his day, when "a poet . . . constantly . . . dazzles his readers. . . . Only that which is startling . . . makes a noise and is talked about." He preferred a poetry that showed "reserve" or modesty. By holding back emotionally, Keble requires readers to enter into the experience of his poems, to make the emotional connections ourselves. His main demand is on our intellect, as we follow his train of thought and unravel his often obscure expression. Keble's poetry does offer its own kind of surprise and freshness, but they arise from its thought, not from its poetic expression.

The Christian Year is subtitled "Thoughts in verse for the Sundays and holydays throughout the year." His stated aim is to bring the reader's feelings into harmony with the Book of Common Prayer. It is an attempt to bring together the personal utterance of the Romantic and Evangelical movements with the more austere liturgical devotion of the Oxford Movement.[1] Each poem in *The Christian Year* has a scriptural text, taken from the Prayer Book readings for the day. Keble usually reads the lesson historically and then finds applications in our own lives, applying Biblical history to the experience of the Christian heart. In these ways his poems resemble sermons.

For Quinquagesima (the Sunday before Lent), the First Lesson at Morning Prayer is Genesis 9, in which, after Noah's flood, God vows never again to destroy the Earth, and as a token of that covenant sets his rainbow in the cloud. Keble's poem is a meditation on the rainbow, which takes us through several stages. As the waters of the flood recede, Noah sets eyes on the rainbow:

> And what most welcome and serene
>   Dawns on the patriarch's eye,
> In all the emerging hills so green,
>   In all the brightening sky?

The Front Quad of Oriel College, Oxford, under a coating of snow. The view takes in the east range, built in 1637-42, with the hall to the left and the ante-chapel to the right. The Gothic style of the windows, antiquated by the seventeenth century, is an example of a long-lived romantic medievalism that contributed to shaping the Oxford Movement.

The last line of the stanza is good, with its brightening vowels, as the rain-clouds clear. Keble regards the rainbow as a softened version of the Sun; it symbolizes what we can see and know of God since we could not endure God's full radiance:

> What but the gentle rainbow's gleam,
>   Soothing the wearied sight,
> That cannot bear the solar beam,
>   With soft undazzling light?

Then, like others before him, Keble plays on the homophones "Sun" and "Son":

> The Son of God in radiance beamed
>   Too bright for us to scan,
> But we may face the rays that streamed
>   From the mild Son of Man.

Keble is paraphrasing the opening of the Epistle to the Hebrews, in which God the Son is "the brightness of [God's] glory." Since we could not look upon that Sun-like brilliance in its heavenly form, God enabled us to look on his Son in earthly form. Christ's human form mediates God's heavenly glory in the same way as the rainbow mediates the full light of the Sun. Next, the rainbow takes on another meaning: we see not only God's brightness but also God's love operate through the different actions, the different colours, of Christ's earthly life.

> There, parted into rainbow hues,
>   In sweet harmonious strife
> We see celestial love diffuse
>   Its light o'er Jesus' life.

Keble ends with a scientific metaphor, based on the prismatic nature of the rainbow. As the several colours of the rainbow are all components of a single white light, so every varied grace that God bestows on us is a partial manifestation of his complete love:

> God, by his bow, vouchsafes to write

> This truth in Heaven above:
> As every lovely hue is light,
> So every grace is love.

The poem for the Tuesday before Easter is one of the few in *The Christian Year* that is unrhymed. Keble thus avoids the awkward inversions of word order that rhyming often forced on him. Its more direct language is one source of this poem's remarkable power. Keble takes his text from the Gospel for the day, the passion narrative of St Mark: "They gave him to drink wine mingled with myrrh: but he received it not." Keble meditates on this refusal. The wine and myrrh are intended to dull Christ's suffering, but Christ refuses to dull it:

> Thou wilt feel all, that thou mayst pity all;
> And rather wouldst thou wreathe[2] with strong pain,
> Than overcloud thy soul,
> So clear in agony,
>
> Or lose one glimpse of Heaven before the time.

Christ's willingness to feel all the suffering that accompanies his death is related to his ability to pity all the suffering sinners for whom he dies. He also models human hope and endurance as he looks to heaven as his only solace and destination. There follows one long slow sentence, which imitates Christ's long slow death on the cross:

> O most entire and perfect sacrifice,
> Renewed in every pulse
> That on the tedious Cross
>
> Told the long hours of death, as, one by one,
> The life-strings of that tender heart gave way;
> E'en sinners, taught by thee,
> Look Sorrow in the face,
>
> And bid her freely welcome, unbeguiled
> By false kind solaces, and spells of earth.

Keble's first teaching for us sinners is that we, too, must confront sorrow or suffering, not disguise it or avoid it by "false kind solaces" or earthly delusions. Then he takes a further step and draws out another teaching. There is solace after all, not through a drug, but because sorrow is transformed into a kind of joy by the power of forgiveness and love:

> And yet not all unsoothed;
> For when was joy so dear,
>
> As the deep calm that breathed, "Father, forgive,"
> Or, "Be with me in Paradise to-day?"
> And, though the strife be sore,
> Yet in his parting breath
>
> Love masters agony; the soul that seemed
> Forsaken, feels her present God again,
> And in her Father's arms
> Contented dies away.

Those fine last six lines convey a mix of dissolving and peacefulness. Keble remembers first the words, "My God, my God, why hast thou forsaken me?" ("the soul that seemed forsaken"). He then remembers the last words, "Father, into thy hands I commend my spirit." He does not directly cite those words, but he expects us to remember them, as Christ's soul "feels her present God again." The artistic form of the *Pietà* depicts the male body of the dead Christ in the arms of the female Virgin Mary. In Keble's version the female soul of Christ dies away in the arms of her father. It is a deathbed scene of the kind that would adorn many a Victorian novel, and that many people of that period would have experienced personally. It gives an image of the oneness of Father and Son, and it offers also a model for how we may hope to die, in faith and love.

Keble's Sermons

The sermon was one of the great forms of religious and literary expression in Keble's day. In the eighteenth and nineteenth centuries "preaching was one, if not the principal, shared experience of all classes and conditions of people."[3] The Oxford Movement aimed to redress the imbalance by which, even in Anglicanism, the importance of the sermon had come to prevail in people's minds over the daily offices and the Eucharist. Nevertheless, much of the impact made by Keble and the Oxford Movement came through their sermons. According to John Henry Newman's over-dramatic story, it was a sermon by Keble that initiated the Oxford Movement.

Keble's ten volumes of *Sermons for the Christian Year* contain more than 500 sermons, and he issued yet more collections. If Keble's poetry may be described as sermons dressed in poetic forms, his sermons have an impassioned eloquence and directness that might be called poetic. Their content was reinforced by their delivery: Newman wrote, "what music there was in the simple earnestness and sweet gravity with which he spoke."[4]

One series of four sermons treats the four "marks" of the church as defined by the Nicene Creed: "one, holy, catholic, and apostolic." Gathered in this "one" church are "all those who are . . . subject to Christ, at all times: both those who are now on their training in this imperfect world, and those who now or hereafter shall be taken up and made perfect in Paradise and in Heaven." This is a splendid vision of the church extending throughout space and time. Keble explains in a simile how these different states of the church can still be one: "Just as the little child in his weakness is nevertheless the same person as the full-grown man in his strength, so the church militant on earth, with its sins and imperfections, is nevertheless the same kingdom with the church made perfect and triumphant in Heaven." This simple but profound illustration is a reminder that most of Keble's sermons were addressed to a country congregation of the mid-nineteenth century. He never patronizes that congregation, but he does take care to express sophisticated ideas in direct clear language.

Keble quotes three Biblical parables that describe the growth of the church on earth: "The grain of mustard-seed . . . sown [on the first Pentecost] has grown into a great tree; the leaven has spread through the whole three measures of meal; the vine brought out of Egypt has had room made for it, it hath waxen great, and filled the earth." Keble's words are simple but vivid, fervent, even prophetic. This church is not just an institution that exists "out there":

> we ourselves are members of this body [literally, limbs of the body], sheep of this fold, branches of this tree, citizens of this kingdom. . . . the meanest beggar, who has been baptized into Christ, is as truly a member of Christ as the greatest king: . . . the mere ordinary Christian . . . is as truly and really in Christ (though much more unworthily), as S. Paul or S. Peter was. It is a strange and fearful thought, but so it is.

Keble describes the gift and dignity of belonging to the body of Christ as a new and miraculous discovery (as indeed it is).

Keble explains that the church is catholic or universal because it exists throughout space and time, but also "by teaching . . . all necessary and saving truth." Keble gives a classic explanation for how this complete or catholic truth is taught by the Anglican church in particular: it "puts . . . the Bible into the hands of each one of us, and says, 'This is the book of God:' it teaches us also the catechism, especially the Creed, and says, 'This is the meaning of God's book, for thus it was understood in the holy ancient church, when all Christians were evidently one body.'" The early Anglican divines originated this principle: to interpret the Bible in the light of the teachings of the early undivided church, which they dated until about the year 500. Keble has no doubt that on this basis the Anglican church teaches the Catholic faith in its entirety. It is all the more important to be grateful for this gift and to hold to it faithfully because of the "perplexities and distresses" of the times and of the church—a point that applies now as it did in Keble's time.

The church is apostolic, because it carries on the mission that Christ gave his apostles, and that has been handed down in a succession that can be traced back to that moment:

> every priest or deacon saying prayers or preaching in church, or visiting the sick, or administering either of the sacraments, or privately reproving or comforting or instructing any in Christ's name, he too is a living and moving token of our Lord's presence. For from some one of the bishops, the apostles' successors, he received a call

> to do these things; and by virtue of our Lord's promise to his apostles, he goes about doing them.

These everyday actions embody and enact the continuing living presence of Christ in his church, to which he promised, "I will be with you always." To teach and to put into practice a revived doctrine of the church as catholic and apostolic was the original aim of the Oxford Movement. Keble develops this teaching comprehensively and forcefully: the kingdom of God, the kingdom of heaven, of which Christ speaks is none other than the church, a church that extends vastly throughout space and time, but is also alive now, among us. The fervent language of Keble's sermons is an Anglican equivalent to great Baroque paintings like *The Triumph of the Church* by Rubens, depicting the cosmic splendour of the universal church.

A final example of Keble's preaching is an Easter Day sermon of 1863, among the last that he delivered. Taking the text, "Come, see the place where the Lord lay," Keble reviews the many meanings of the empty tomb. Using one of the traditional techniques of meditation, Keble invites us to visualize a vivid final scene at the tomb and to make ourselves present there:

> It is early, just after sunrise on the Sunday morning: . . . [with] two women, elderly persons both of them . . . look well upon this cave, here lying open before you: . . . See the place where thy Lord lay, where he laid himself down of his own free will, and be ashamed of thy pride and high looks.

First, then, a teaching of humility; second, a test of faith, for us as for the women: " 'Come,' is the divine message: 'come see, not at once your risen Lord himself, but the place where he lay. His will is to try and prove you, whether you will believe without seeing, that your blessing may be the greater when you are permitted to see.'"

Keble then switches from Matthew's words to Mark's, and—a third teaching—we are present in a different way. It is our own sinfulness (now) that crucified Christ (then):

> "behold the place where *they laid him*," mark, not "where he lay," but "where they laid him:" by which words we are put in mind not so much of our Lord's humbling himself

as of the spite and cruelty of his enemies, who laid him low. And who, and what are they? Not the Jews and Pilate only, but we, my brethren, we Christians, we and our worldly unchristian ways.

Fourth: "The whole earth has been from that day forward the place where Jesus lay for a time, where he lived and breathed, was born and died, ate and drank, slept and waked, moved and talked, did and suffered." Keble introduces an emphasis on the Incarnation that would become a distinctive feature of Catholic Anglicanism. By becoming flesh, God honoured human nature and our Earth. We do not therefore regard human nature solely as fallen, innately given to sin (though that is part of the truth); we remember also that we are made in God's image, and that God the Son assumed our nature. We see in our neighbour the image of God and of Christ, which is why, from the ministries of Herbert and Law to those of the slum priests in London and elsewhere, Catholic Anglicanism has set so much store by ministry to the outcast and marginalized. Or, in Keble's remarkable words:

> no soul, or body of man can ever be looked on or thought of . . . as it might have been if God had not vouchsafed to become Incarnate, and die for it. Since that day, you and I and every one born into the world of the seed of Adam is a real blood relation . . . to Jesus Christ the Son of God.

For Keble the tomb viewed on Easter Day shows the darkness of a humankind that crucified Christ, but also promises his continuing presence among us. This truth is captured in a vivid final image:

> His having been once here is our token that he is always here in heart. The moment you turn to him in earnest . . . there he is, there you find him, watching as it were to catch your eye, feeling for you, and with you, with a true heart's love.

This image may remember Exodus, when "the Lord spake unto Moses face to face, as a man speaketh unto his friend." It also suggests not only that Christ is like a friend, catching your eye across a room or across the street, but that a friend embodies Christ.

Endnotes

[1] It might be said that the Oxford Movement originated when the Book of Common Prayer met the nature romanticism of William Wordsworth's poetry and the historical romanticism of Walter Scott's novels.

[2] "Wreathe" here means twist, contort, writhe, a meaning still in use in Keble's time.

[3] Keith A. Francis et al., eds, *The Oxford Handbook of the British Sermon 1689-1901* (Oxford: Oxford University Press, 2012), p. xiii.

[4] Quoted by E. B. Pusey, in *Occasional Papers and Reviews by John Keble* (Oxford and London: James Parker, 1877), p. xiv.

Further Reading

Georgina Battiscombe, *John Keble: a study in limitations*. London: Constable, 1963.

Charles R. Henery, ed., *A Speaking Life: John Keble and the Anglican tradition of ministry and art*. Leominster, Heref.: Gracewing, 1995.

See also the further reading for the Oxford Movement, below.

John Henry Newman, a stipple engraving by Richard Woodman (1784-1859), after a miniature by William Charles Ross (1794-1860). The miniature dates from c. 1845, the year in which Newman joined the Roman Catholic church. The portrait communicates the authority and the intensity that won Newman great personal allegiance and helped make him the accepted leader of the Oxford Movement.

9

Tracts for the Times
Theology of the Church

The Tracts for the Times were a series of pamphlets and books published between 1833 and 1841. They were the founding manifesto of modern Catholic Anglicanism, and had a shaping influence on later Anglicanism in general. The dramatic story of the Tractarian movement, now more generally known as the Oxford Movement, has often been told: its beginnings in the Assize Sermon of John Keble in 1833; its gathering strength in the later 1830s under the leadership of John Henry Newman; the extremes of allegiance and opposition it attracted, centred on Oxford but spreading well beyond; the storm of controversy in 1841 over Newman's Tract 90, on the Thirty-Nine Articles—the final Tract as it turned out; Newman's conversion to Roman Catholicism in 1845.

This chapter examines the subject at the heart of the Tracts, the nature of the church and the idea of the Catholic. From the Tractarians' theology of the church in general, the following chapter traces their particular understanding of the place of the Anglican Church within Christendom. These remain their great contribution to questions of doctrine. The Tractarians' vision of the church as the body of Christ, with its antiquity reaching back to Christ himself, with its power to unite, to heal, and to encourage, is still able to inspire the reader of the Tracts. The Tractarians were also admired for giving expression and vitality to doctrine through conduct; in other words, for their spirituality, their example of living out the Christian life. That aspect is the subject of the third chapter on the Tracts. The three chapters together carry through the two structuring themes of this book: the nature and importance of the church, and of the Anglican church in particular; and living out the Christian life, concerning which we have already read much impressive Anglican teaching.

A "tract" was a cheap pamphlet, a humble form of publication, then as now more associated with fringe groups than with learned Oxford dons, who penned the Tracts for the Times.[1] To write tracts was a way of saying that here was something that needed to be published quickly and distributed widely, that the times did not allow the luxury of studied composition or leisurely exposition. Hence, ninety of these tracts were published in seven years; the first seventy-seven in three years. At first, there was a barrage of short tracts published in rapid succession, as a way of putting the new movement on the public scene and gaining maximum attention. With time, the tracts became less frequent and much longer: having caught attention and mobilized energy in the short term, they then seek to solidify the structure of Catholic Anglicanism for the long term. Where the earlier tracts are usually eight or twelve pages long, the last twenty tracts are usually about sixty pages, and a few are much longer: Edward Bouverie Pusey's Tract 67, "Scriptural Views of Holy Baptism," an argument supporting the doctrine of baptismal regeneration, runs to 400 pages in its revised printings.

Most of the Tracts are new compositions; some are, however, selections from writings by the early church Fathers and by early Anglican writers, especially from the seventeenth century. In this way, the Tractarians wish to show that their aim of restoring the Catholic element of Anglican tradition does not teach anything novel but is part of a long tradition. Newman evokes this tradition beautifully when he writes of "the memory of our great teachers, champions, and confessors, now in Paradise, especially of those of the seventeenth century,—Hammond's name alone, were there no other, or Hooker's, or Ken's,—bind us to the Anglican Church, by cords of love" (Tract 71).[2] An example of these reprints is the immensely long Tract 81, running to 424 pages in its second edition, and also probably largely the work of Pusey. This Tract is a "catena" or an anthology of the *Testimony of Writers in the Later English Church to the Doctrine of the Eucharistic Sacrifice*; it reprints extracts from sixty-three writers, from John Jewel in the sixteenth century to Henry Phillpotts, Bishop of Exeter at the time of the Tracts. Many of these writings were forgotten or difficult of access in the 1830s, so the Tractarians are restoring them to circulation, a project comparable to posting material on the internet today.[3] The present book has a similar aim, albeit on a far more modest scale.

A series of tracts allowed a variety of authors. The majority had a connection with Oriel College, Oxford. In the first half of the nineteenth century, Oriel experienced a brilliant efflorescence, and the Tracts for the Times reflect the intellectual and ethical vigour of that environment. Notwithstanding the principle of anonymous publication, it is not difficult to detect the differing voices and emphases that the main writers contribute to the series. John Henry Newman (1809-1890), the most active figure in launching the Tracts, has the most agile mind of the Tractarians. This agility is often stimulating, if at times overdone: Newman can read like a clever lawyer who will argue anything to win his case.[4] This characteristic in their leading writer helped produce the mistrust with which the Tracts were greeted in many quarters. Edward Bouverie Pusey (1800-1882) was responsible for expanding the Tracts from brief pamphlets to longer, fully argued treatises, and so imparting a greater *gravitas* to the movement. Pusey was Regius Professor of Hebrew at Oxford, and his Tracts are nothing if not professorial. He rarely makes a statement without quoting three or four authorities to support it; he is the most laborious of the writers.[5] Keble, by contrast, often cultivates a homely style, preferring a gentler form of persuasion from probability and domestic analogies, a manner recognizable from his sermons. Keble and his brother, Thomas, contribute the imaginary dialogues between a Tractarian clergyman and Richard Nelson, "a respectable young working man" and Sunday school teacher, who, in his humble but sensible way, has miraculously arrived at all the same conclusions as the learned Tractarians.

The Tracts for the Times began as a response to the reforming intentions of the Whig ministry of Earl Grey, which had taken office in 1830. Having repaired, or begun to repair, the defective electoral system amid heated controversy in 1832, the ministry was now turning its attention to the Church of England, in a spirit similar to that shown by the Whig government in the time of Bishop Benjamin Hoadly. Like other institutions of the time, the church had serious organizational defects, some of them amounting to corruption. Clergy with influential social connections could hold multiple livings, often wealthy ones, while farming out the actual work to humble curates on low pay. Bishops lived like lords from the proceeds of church revenues: the Archbishop of Canterbury, William Howley (1766-1848), would leave a fortune of £120,000, a huge sum at the time, largely acquired through patronage. There was also a considerable degree of indolence in the way some clergy carried out, or failed to carry out, their duties.[6] All this the Tractarians readily admitted and deplored. Newman laments the willingness of clergy to abuse church buildings, "To board over the altar of a church, place an orchestra there of playhouse singers, and take money at the doors" (Tract 41). Pusey laments that "we . . . have brought down our celebrations of the Communion from weekly to monthly, or quarterly, or three times in the year; . . . and have lost (for the most part) the very sense and feeling, that more frequent communion would be a blessing" (Tract 81).

What the Tractarians did not admit was that a secular government had the right to legislate for church affairs, no matter how tainted they might be. The first four Tracts, as well as later ones, sound an alarm at the political threat to the church through the possibility of revision of the Prayer Book or perhaps even doctrinal interference, all from a Parliament that was no longer Anglican and might not much longer even be Christian.[7] Rioting at the time of the Reform Bills had targeted bishops and their palaces, since it was well known that the Church of England generally opposed even moderate political reform.[8] This situation gave rise to lurid fears on the part of the Tractarians, based on memories of the French Revolution, on an exaggerated view of the more recent July Revolution of 1830 in France, and on the supposed perfidy of the Whig party. In Tract 23, A. P. Perceval warns that churchmen must expect to suffer persecution, "as we suffered together with good King Charles at the hands of the Dissenters; as we suffered in the days of bloody Queen Mary, at the hands of the Roman Catholics; as we suffered during the first three hundred years after Christ, at the hands of the heathens and the Jews." In Tract 10, Newman foresees the spoliation of the church and the degradation of its priests:

> Time was, when they were even persecuted, cruelly slain by fire and sword. That time, (though God avert it!) may come again. But, whether or not Satan is permitted so openly to rage, certainly some kinds of persecution are to be expected in our day; nay, such have begun. It is not so very long since the great men of the earth told them to *prepare for persecution*; it is not so very long since the mad people answered the summons, and furiously attacked them, and seemed bent on destroying them, in all parts of the country.
>
> Yes! the day may come, even in this generation, when the representatives of Christ are spoiled of their sacred possessions, and degraded from their civil dignities. The day may come, when each of us inferior ministers . . . may have to give up our churches . . . Then you will honour us, . . . as those (if I may say so) who are intrusted with the keys of heaven and hell, as the heralds of mercy, as the denouncers of woe to wicked men, as intrusted with the awful and mysterious privilege of dispensing Christ's body and blood, as far greater than the most powerful and the wealthiest of men in our unseen strength and our heavenly riches.

In the face of this menace, largely imaginary but not impossible, Newman asserts the fundamental premise of the Tracts for the Times, the doctrine that the Tractarians set out to revive for the church of their time. The authority of the Anglican priesthood derives not from social position or politically motivated appointment but from the apostolic succession, and the apostolic succession is, in turn, Christ's own chosen foundation for his church. This doctrine is expounded in many Tracts and in many voices: in Newman's prophetic exhortation to his fellow priests (Tract 1), in Keble's gentle urging that we seek to please Christ by respecting his will (Tract 4), in the earnest inquiry of Richard Nelson, Keble's imaginary young working man, as he sifts the Biblical and historical evidence (Tract 12). It is given magisterial expression in Newman's catena of Anglican authorities, for the instruction of fellow Anglicans who do not understand the importance of the apostolic succession:

> Christ founded a visible church as an ordinance for ever, and endowed it once for all with spiritual privileges, and set his apostles over it, as the first in a line of ministers and rulers, like themselves except in their miraculous gifts, and to be continued from them by successive ordination; in consequence, ... to adhere to this church thus distinguished, is among the ordinary duties of a Christian (Tract 74).

The church therefore has an independent and powerful authority of its own, which cannot be usurped by the state.

Quoting John Pearson's *Exposition of the Creed* (1659), Newman's Tract 2 gives to the church a central role in salvation: "Christ hath appointed it as the only way to eternal life." This Tract further explains that

> Almighty God might have left Christianity as a sort of sacred literature, as contained in the Bible, which each person was to take and use by himself; ... but, in matter of fact, he has ordained otherwise. He has actually set up a society, which exists even this day all over the world, and which (as a general rule) Christians are bound to join; so that to believe in Christ is not a mere opinion or a secret conviction, but a social or even a political principle.[9]

For the recipients of the apostolic succession within the church, it is the fact of this reception, their office as bishop or priest or deacon, that matters. Unworthy individuals will on occasion fill those offices, but their unworthiness will not cancel their role. Newman explains this through the simile of a dispensary or pharmacy: "as we betake ourselves to a dispensary for medicine, without attributing praise or intrinsic worth to the building or the immediate managers of its stores, in something of the like manner we are to come to that one society, to which Christ has entrusted the office of stewardship in the distribution of gifts, of which he alone is the author and real dispenser" (Tract 11). The efficacy of the medicine depends on the inventor or manufacturer, not the retailer. This understanding is different from the Evangelical emphasis on the individual, "this or that distinguished preacher." It also means that the Roman Church was able to pass on the apostolic succession despite its errors (Tract 15, William Palmer). Priests should therefore be wholehearted in their claim to come as "ambassadors for Christ" (a term taken from 2 Corinthians 5:20), not for their own aggrandizement but for the reassurance of the people to whom they minister (Tract 17, Benjamin Harrison).

The church is designed to be "one." Unity being essential, it is a sin to separate from the main body, as dissenters in England had done. This is a hint of the stern and inflexible side of Tractarianism. Nevertheless, at least in the early stages of the Tracts, Newman believed that it was possible to combine a true doctrine of the church with an Evangelical posture. To a real or imaginary Evangelical friend, Newman writes that he is "not asking you at present to abandon your own opinions, but to add to them a practical belief in a tenet which the Creed teaches and Scripture has consecrated." Newman believes this to be possible, mentioning the case of an unnamed clergyman who was "both a Calvinist, and a strenuous high-churchman" (Tract 11). Be that as it may—and there is little further mention in the Tracts of such a reconciliation—a vague idea of the church is not enough. The church cannot be what Protestants are too willing to accept, "a mere number of good people scattered over the world, who may or may not have communion with each other . . . but one public, orderly, visible body, consisting of ministers and people, such as the Church of England" (Tract 29, J. W. Bowden). Therefore, "Christian liberty" is not a justification for joining any congregation or keeping up any form of worship one pleases. Since God has enjoined us to join the one Catholic Church, "The true liberty wherewith Christ has made us free, is theirs alone, who in reverencing his ministers, walk in the way of his commandments" (Tract 30, J. W. Bowden).

The Tractarians base their theology of the church on the Bible and on the practice of the Apostles and the early church, but they also, following the Anglican tradition established by Hooker, show how it conforms to reason and human psychology. With bishops taking the position of commanders and spokesmen, a hierarchy makes better organizational sense than a scattering of independently acting parsons (Tract 3, Newman). The visible church is a source of assurance against doubt or discouragement:

> How cheering it is to a person . . . to be able to point to others elsewhere, who actually hold the same opinions as himself, and exert themselves for the same objects! Why? because it is an appeal to a *fact*, which no one can deny; it is an evidence that the view which influences him is something external to his own mind, and not a dream. (Tract 20, Newman)

No less than Scripture, the ceremonies of the church are a means of teaching and perpetuating the essential doctrines of Christianity: they are "the outward forms which God himself has appointed to arrest our attention, to embody unseen realities, to serve as a kind of ladder between earth and heaven." Even in times when truth is not fully understood or universally followed, the sacraments continue to witness to it: "*something* is living on, . . . independent of the variable opinions of the human mind" (Tract 32, C. P. Eden).

An impressive summary of the importance of the church in the totality of Christian doctrine and experience is given by Isaac Williams in Tract 87:

> each article in the third part of the [Apostles'] Creed, respecting the dispensation of the Spirit, is found fulfilled in the church after a living manner. . . . "The Holy Catholic Church" is realized throughout it, all our principles and practices being thence derived, and holding us in union with her. "The Communion of Saints" is maintained by unity of worship, by similarity of devotional forms, by one baptism, and also by her saints' days; whereby various churches throughout the world, by commemorating the

same saints, on the same days, preserve a communion of spirit with the living, and also with the dead, whom they commemorate. "The Forgiveness of sins," is taught by her sacraments, and absolution. "The Resurrection of the body," by the doctrine of the Eucharist, ... and the whole tone of her liturgy and prayers, looks forward to "a life everlasting after death." So fully do her services contain every doctrine and every principle which has a reference to the Holy Spirit.

The rediscovery of the centrality of the church, the Tractarians believed, has an effect comparable to the Copernican revolution in science. In the earthly organization of our religious life we had become accustomed to a Ptolemaic system, our Protestantism, in which religious experience is centred on our small individual selves. The Copernican discovery of our Catholic nature means that the central place is occupied by the great light-giving source of the church and that individual lives find their place in relation to that sun. This discovery in no way diminishes us; on the contrary, it elevates us by making us part of something vastly greater than our separate selves (Tract 49, B. Harrison). Another striking simile for recovery of the Catholic doctrine of the church is drawn from the science of archaeology that was coming into existence at the time of the Tracts for the Times: "Thus the consecrated form of religion will be like some fair statue, which lies buried for ages, but comes forth at length as beautiful as ever" (Tract 32, C. P. Eden).[10]

A persuasive argument for the authority of the church is the fact that there are important Christian doctrines or practices that cannot be traced directly or fully to Christ's teaching or injunction, or even to specific Biblical example. In these cases, all Christians, whether they know it or not, rely on the authority of the early church and the traditions that it has passed on. In Tract 45, Newman points out that neither the doctrine of the Trinity nor the practice of infant baptism is formally stated or enjoined in Scripture. Therefore, as to infant baptism: "Why do we observe it? Because the primitive church observed it." Likewise, "Where (*e.g.*) are we told in Scripture, that gambling is wrong? or again, suicide?"

In this cartoon of unknown origin, probably dating from 1865, the three central figures are the three leaders of the Oxford Movement, Pusey, Newman, and Keble. Newman is holding a copy of his autobiographical *Apologia pro vita sua* (1864), Keble a copy of *The Christian Year* (1827). At left is H. E. Manning, who was allied with the Movement and contributed to one of the Tracts for the Times. Like Newman, Manning eventually joined the Roman Catholic church and is pictured wearing his robes as Archbishop of Westminster. Manning became a cardinal in 1875, Newman in 1879. At right is Samuel Wilberforce, Bishop of Oxford, never a part of the Movement and often opposed to it. All except Manning were members of Oriel College, Oxford.

In Tract 78, Henry Manning and Charles Marriott add other commonly received fundamentals of Christianity that derive from tradition, including the canon of Scripture itself and the observance of Sunday.[11] In Tract 34, Newman notes that there is only "a solitary allusion in Scripture to houses of prayer under the Christian system, which nevertheless we know from ecclesiastical history were used from the very first." These examples are also important when discussion turns to Scriptural authority for the organization of the clergy into the degrees of bishops, priests, and deacons. If this organization is not explicitly mandated by Scripture, the same is true of other important doctrines and practices. As in those cases, so with episcopacy and hierarchy: "we are bound to venerate what is certainly primitive, and probably is apostolic" (Tract 34). The way in which the authority of the Scriptures is in these cases supplemented by the authority of the church establishes that the Scriptures "constitute a rule of *faith*, not a rule of *practice*; a rule of *doctrine*, not a rule of *conduct* or *discipline*" (Tract 45). Hooker had arrived at a similar conclusion.

The nature and role of the church was a question of urgency for the Tractarians, because they believed that these matters had been neglected by the Anglicanism of the preceding century. The question is alive again in our own time and place, with a revived Evangelicalism discarding much in the traditional understanding of the church. The Tracts controvert many of the doctrines and attitudes of this movement. One is the assumption that the New Law has superseded institutions and ceremonies, which are the mark of the Old Law merely, that the corporal has given way, or should give way, to the spiritual. In Tract 32, C. P. Eden interrogates this assumption with pertinence and eloquence:

> 1. Are we quite sure that *we* are more spiritual, and more independent of the external helps of the church, than Samuel,—Hezekiah,—Josiah,—and Daniel?— 2. What does our own experience say? Do we see the best and holiest of men becoming most independent and regardless of them, or the very reverse? 3. . . . Are not the ordinances which Christ and his apostles have appointed, the *bond of perpetuated unity* to the church, a precious and mysteri-

> ous medium for the "communion of saints" in all countries and ages? ... And is it not a soothing and elevating privilege, to feel that we, even at this distant day, are allowed to come and walk in the very steps of all the holy men of old, the glorious company of the apostles, and the noble army of martyrs, to take that narrow path, whose farther end they have now found to be in heaven? ... and is it no privilege, no blessing, to *think* with him, to have our spirit admitted to move in the same path which his Holy Spirit hath chosen; to be consecrated with him and to him in the water of baptism, to eat the Holy Supper with him, to fast with him, to pray with him in the very form and very thoughts which flowed from his divine mind and lips?

Pusey, too, diagnoses a kind of spiritual pride in elevating private judgement over the authority of the church: "we have been accustomed to do, 'every one that which was right in his own eyes,' and are jealous of any authority, except that of the direct injunctions of the Bible: in extolling also the spirituality of our religion, we have, I fear, intended covertly to panegyrise our own" (Tract 18).

Newman in Tract 7 puts his finger on the logical consequences of doing away with apostolic authority. His example is the claim of non-episcopal churches, which have broken the chain of apostolic succession, to ordain ministers by the laying on of hands. He points out that this claim can depend only on individual authority, not on a commission that can be traced through the Apostles to Christ:

> If they may ordain without being sent to do so, others may teach and preach without being sent. They hold a middle position, which is untenable as destroying itself; for if Christians do without bishops (i.e., commissioned ordainers), they may do without commissioned ministers (i.e., the priests and deacons). If an imposition of hands is necessary to convey one gift, why should it not be to convey another?

Likewise in the matter of "lay presidency": if unordained people can administer sacraments, why are ordained people needed to teach and preach?

Isaac Williams, in his magnificent Tract 87, mounts a powerful defence of Catholic tradition, its visible church, its bishops and priests, its sacraments and offices, its emphasis on both faith and works, and delivers also a powerful critique of the single-mindedness of an Evangelical system based on the atonement and preaching. According to the Evangelical emphasis on preaching, writes Williams, "the church of God would be the house of preaching; but Scripture calls it the house of prayer." The Evangelical system works on the principle

> that it is necessary to obtrude and "bring forward *prominently* and *explicitly* on all occasions the doctrine of the Atonement." This one thing it puts in the place of all the principles held by the Church Catholic, dropping all proportion of the faith. It disparages comparatively, nay, in some cases has even blasphemed, the most blessed sacraments. It is very jealously afraid of church authority, of fasting and mortification being recommended, of works of holiness being insisted on, of the doctrine of the universal judgment.... In fact, this system is nothing else but a method of human device, which is able to quote a part of Scripture for its purpose. It is not according to the general tenor or the analogy of Scripture, nor is it founded or based on Scripture as its origin.

Williams agrees that it is of the highest importance that the hearts of Christians should be instilled with a sense of Christ's atonement:

> But how is this state to be obtained? These peculiar opinions are formed on the supposition, that it is by declaring these truths aloud to all we meet. This is the point on which we are at issue. For this we think there is no sanction in all the laws of our moral nature and religious philosophy; that there is none for it in the Catholic Church, none in Holy Scripture.

The Evangelical system "puts knowledge first, and obedience afterwards: let this doctrine, they say, be received, and good works will necessarily follow. Holy Scripture throughout adopts the opposite course." Williams vindicates the role of works as a means of leading the soul to receive God, and of giving an example to others:

He who most of all practises these duties, will be most of all brought, by a necessary and moral consequence, to value the Cross of Christ ... He, therefore, who most of all induces men to practise these good works, under the awful sense of their condition as baptized Christians, brings them most of all to the Cross of Christ; and he who, by his teaching, leads men to think that such works are of minor importance, and speaks slightingly of them, i.e., works of charity, of humiliation, and prayer, teaches men false and dangerous doctrine, flattering to human indolence, but opposed to Scripture, opposed to the church, opposed to the first principles of our moral nature.

Endnotes

[1] In England, a wave of pamphlet publication took place around the Civil War period: the London bookseller George Thomason collected 22,000 pamphlets printed in the period 1640-1661. In the USA, the *Federalist Papers* of 1787-1788, which advocated the ratification of the Constitution, have points of comparison with the Tracts for the Times. Both were the work of a group of writers of some eminence, who did not name themselves; both were written in the first instance to support a particular cause; both have proved to have a lasting interest, wider and deeper than their original occasion.

Tracts for the Times is a term describing a series, each with its own title. For that reason, I do not print Tract for the Times in italics. Likewise Tract 90 (for example) identifies the particular tract, but is not its title, and therefore I do not print such identifiers in italics.

[2] In naming the authors of the Tracts, most of which were published anonymously, I follow Rune Imberg, *In Quest of Authority* (Lund, Sweden: Lund University Press, 1987), Appendix I, which reviews all sources of information on the topic. The writers to whom Newman accords such reverence are, in addition to Richard Hooker, Henry Hammond (1605-1660), who wrote influential defences of episcopacy and acted as chaplain to King Charles I during the Civil War, and Thomas Ken (1637-1711), a Nonjuror in 1688, who wrote devotional writings, including *The Practice of Divine Love* (1685).

[3] Owen Chadwick makes another comparison: "they set out to make the

Fathers available to the English reader, with something of the same religious spirit in which the Reformers had sought to make the Bible available in the language of the people", *The Spirit of the Oxford Movement: Tractarian essays* (Cambridge: Cambridge University Press, 1990), p. 30.

⁴ Newman shows himself aware of this tendency, when he writes about the temptation of "an over-desire to convince others, or, in other words a desire to out-argue others" (Tract 19). Hooker's arguments are also occasionally forced.

⁵ A fuller and perhaps more respectful description of Pusey's style is the following: "To the tractarians, the manner reflected the solemnity of the matter with which they were concerned. Pusey . . . cared nothing for grace of expression, achieved lucidity not without an effort, but was the heir of the dignity of the ancient divines. He was a master of serried argument, repeating his blows as with a hammer, cogent, cumulative, compelling, if not convincing, to assent, rarely epigrammatic, never concise." W. H. Hutton, "The Oxford Movement," *Cambridge History of English and American Literature*, ed. A. W. Ward et al. (Cambridge: Cambridge University Press, 1907-1921), Volume 12, Chapter 12, par 18.

⁶ Modern research has corrected the looser and exaggerated descriptions of clerical negligence that prevailed among earlier historians of the Oxford Movement. See, for example, Gordon Rupp, *Religion in England, 1688-1791* (Oxford: Clarendon Press, 1986), and John Walsh, Colin Haydon, and Stephen Taylor, *The Church of England, c.1689-c.1833: from toleration to Tractarianism* (Cambridge: Cambridge University Press, 1993). The Barsetshire novels of Anthony Trollope give a lively if somewhat later depiction of the state of the church and of movements to reform it.

⁷ The repeal of the Test Acts (1828) and the Catholic Relief Act (1829) had recently opened Parliament to Dissenters and Catholics. It was still necessary for MPs to swear opposition to various political claims of the papacy, real or imaginary. MPs were required to swear a religious oath until 1888.

⁸ The bishops in the House of Lords voted 21-2 against the failed Reform Bill in 1831. Twelve bishops did eventually vote in favour of the successful Reform Bill in 1832.

⁹ Almost any topic in the Tracts leads back to the nature and role of the church. A sermon on the annunciation leads to the incarnation, which leads to the role of orthodox bishops in maintaining this doc-

trine against various heresies in the early history of the church (Tract 54, Keble); conversely, the Tracts argue that churches that discarded the apostolic succession are also likely to have diluted the doctrine of the incarnation (Tract 57, Keble).

[10] Tract 32 was published in 1834. The Institute of Archaeological Correspondence (*Instituto di corrispondenza archeologica* or *Institut für archäologische Korrespondenz*) had been founded in 1829 and began publishing its bulletin and annals. In 1829 the Ashmolean Museum at Oxford had also received its first major collection of archaeological material, the Douglas collection of Anglo-Saxon antiquities from Kent.

[11] Manning, a near contemporary of Newman, followed him in joining the Roman Catholic church, where he became Archbishop of Westminster. Both Manning and Newman became cardinals.

Further Reading (Chapters 9-11)

John Henry Newman, *Apologia pro vita sua* [1864] *and Six Sermons*, ed. Frank M. Turner. New Haven, Conn., and London: Yale University Press, 2008. This is an important scholarly edition of Newman's autobiographical classic. A more accessible edition is: *Apologia pro vita sua*, ed. Ian Ker. Harmondsworth, M'sex: Penguin, 1994.

R. W. Church, *The Oxford Movement: twelve years, 1833–1845*. London: Macmillan, 1891.

Geoffrey Rowell. *The Vision Glorious: themes and personalities of the Catholic revival in Anglicanism*. Oxford: Oxford University Press, 1983.

Owen Chadwick, *The Spirit of the Oxford Movement: Tractarian essays*. Cambridge: Cambridge University Press, 1990.

Peter Benedict Nockles, *The Oxford Movement in Context: Anglican high churchmanship, 1760-1857*. Cambridge: Cambridge University Press, 1994.

James Pereiro, *Ethos and the Oxford Movement: at the heart of Tractarianism*. Oxford: Oxford University Press, 2008.

C. Brad Faught, *The Oxford Movement: a thematic history of the Tractarians and their times*. University Park, Pa.: Penn State University Press, 2003.

10

Tracts for the Times

The Catholic Nature of the Anglican Church

Having reinstated the Catholic church to its place at the centre of Christian life, the Tractarians sought to vindicate what they viewed as the true but neglected catholicity of the Church of England. This emphasis becomes more marked from around the date of Tract 35 in 1834. The term, "Anglo-Catholic", first appears, I believe, only in Newman's final Tract 90, in 1841. That was also the year in which the Oxford bookseller J. H. Parker began publishing the series, "The Library of Anglo-Catholic Theology". That collection, eventually consisting of ninety-five volumes by twenty writers, most of them divines of the sixteenth and seventeenth centuries, set out to consolidate the work of the Tracts for the Times by returning to circulation writings that demonstrated the longevity, intellectual cogency, and spiritual treasure of the Catholic tradition in Anglicanism.

As the Tracts for the Times argued that the basis of the church is the apostolic succession, so they argued that the Anglican church is a direct inheritor of that succession. In Tract 15, the noted liturgical scholar, William Palmer, in his sole contribution to the Tracts, makes this historical case in impressive terms. In separating from Rome, the Anglican church did not reject or lose the apostolic succession. The Reformation was carried out by the church in England itself, by bishops who had received and who passed on the apostolic succession:

> it is certain that the bishops and clergy in England and Ireland remained the same as before the separation, and that it was these, with the aid of the civil power, who de-

livered the church of those kingdoms from the yoke of papal tyranny and usurpation ... The church then by its proper rulers and officers reformed itself. There was no new church founded among us, but the rights and the true doctrines of the ancient existing church were asserted and established.[1]

A similar history is outlined by J. W. Bowden in Tract 30. Both versions surely understate the role of the English crown and Parliament in the English Reformation, and the degree to which the English Reformation had a political as well as a religious basis, but that does not invalidate their main point about the continuity of the church, especially through the medium of the apostolic succession. In Tract 82, a defence of the Tractarians' own continuity with earlier Anglican tradition, Newman summarizes the claims of Anglicanism with simple grandeur: "our apostolical communion inherits, as the promises, so the faith, enjoyed by the saints in every age; the faith which Ignatius, Cyprian, and Gregory received from the apostles. We did not begin on a new foundation in King Edward's time; we only reformed, or repaired, the superstructure."

It is true that the Thirty-Nine Articles, with their strongly Protestant appearance, are part of the heritage of the English church, but no less so are the teachings received from the early church. Newman's Tract 38 describes this rich inheritance in splendid jewelled prose:

> I cannot consent, I am sure the Reformers did not wish me, to deprive myself of the church's dowry, the doctrines which the apostles spoke in Scripture and impressed upon the early church. I receive the church as a messenger from Christ, rich in treasures old and new, rich with the accumulated wealth of ages.... Our Articles are one portion of that accumulation.... As I will not consent to be deprived of the records of the Reformation, so neither will I part with those of former times.

In claiming the mantle of the Catholic, the need for a clear definition of the term becomes apparent. This is supplied in Tract 78, a "Catena Patrum," or a chain of texts by earlier writers, assembled by

The entrance porch of the University Church of St Mary the Virgin, Oxford. An early example of Baroque style in England, the porch was added to the medieval church in 1637. Attesting to the Catholic traditions of Oxford Anglicanism, its statue of the Virgin and Child was the object of Puritan condemnation. Newman was Vicar of St Mary the Virgin, 1828-43, and the impact of the sermons he preached there was widely attested.

H. E. Manning and Charles Marriott. The catena gathers together the "Testimony of writers in the later English church to the duty of maintaining, *Quod semper, quod ubique, quod ab omnibus traditum est.*" This title quotes the famous definition of the term "Catholic" by Vincent of Lérins in the fifth century. The Catholic faith, says Vincent, is "what has been taught always, everywhere, and by all." This definition is simply a felicitous expansion of the Greek word, *katholikos*, which means universal, general.

Vincent's formula is alluded to in Jewel's *Apology* (see p. 37), and Jewel is the first writer quoted in the catena. After Tract 78, the formula is frequently invoked. Newman expands and explicates it in Tract 79:

> it can only be an article of faith, supposing it is held by Antiquity, and that unanimously. For such things only are we allowed to maintain, as come to us from the apostles; and that only (ordinarily speaking) has evidence of so originating, which is witnessed by a number of independent witnesses in the early church. We must have the unanimous "consent of Doctors," as an assurance that the apostles have spoken.

What this means in practice is summed up in the catena of Tract 78 by the eighteenth-century bishop, Thomas Brett: the baseline for Catholic teaching, so to speak, is the doctrines and usages of the time of Nicaea, the last time when the church was fully united. Brett means by this the second Council of Nicaea of 787, not the first of 325, at which the Nicene Creed was promulgated. The second Council of Nicaea was the seventh ecumenical council, and the last attended by the Orthodox churches. The period of the seven councils may therefore be regarded as the period in which doctrines could have been truly held "always, everywhere, and by all."[2] If that is so, then the Anglican church may claim to maintain that Catholic faith more completely than the Protestant churches and more purely than the Roman Catholic church.

By its combination of reform with continuity, argue the Tractarians, the Anglican church has avoided the extremes and the errors of

Protestantism on the one side and Roman Catholicism on the other. In other words, the Anglican church follows a "middle way," in Latin, a *via media*, between extremes. It was in 1834, in Tract 38, that Newman introduced this term to describe the Anglican position. It is easy to suppose that *via media* means a path of caution and compromise: take a little from here and a little from there; do not offend this side and do not offend that. Anglicanism can be caricatured in this fashion. But the remarkably high claims that the Tractarians make for the Catholic character and inheritance of the Anglican church show that the *via media* really means something positive and startlingly assertive.

The Anglican church treads the narrow path of Catholic truth between two broad paths of error. On the one side, Protestantism (including elements within the Anglican church) has subtracted from the Catholic faith by discarding the apostolic succession and by slighting the central importance of the sacraments; on the other side, Roman Catholicism has added features such as the supremacy of the pope, the doctrine of purgatory, and compulsory private confession. It can be shown that the teachings rejected by Protestants did exist, and that those added by the Romans did not exist, in the early church, so both groups fail the test of Vincent, as summarized by Newman; they do not hold to the beliefs that were "held by antiquity, and that unanimously."

As they propound the *via media*, the Tractarians take on a prophetic tone, designating the English nation as a chosen people, a new Israel. In Tract 81, Pusey writes of "the remarkable circumstances of our church, placed as the single guardian of Catholic truth of the West" and exults in the fact that "the peculiarity of our reformation corresponded with the place assigned to us by God's providence, as an island-people, and both with God's blessing; 'This people shall dwell alone, and shall not be reckoned among the nations'" (quoting Numbers 23:9, and thus making England successor to Israel). In Tract 20, Newman extends his prophetic gaze to a global Anglicanism:

> I do believe it to be one most conspicuous mark of God's adorable providence over us, as great as if we saw a mir-

> acle, that Christians in England escaped in the evil day from either extreme ... Thus in every quarter of the world, from North America, to New South Wales, ... he has wonderfully preserved our church as a true branch of the church universal, yet withal preserved it free from doctrinal error. It is Catholic and apostolic, yet not papistical.

At such moments, the Tractarians echo the claims of Hooker (see above, p. 55). They also become the mirror image of the seventeenth-century Puritans at the time of the Civil War. In 1644, John Milton prophesied that "God is decreeing to begin some new and great period in his church, even to the reforming of Reformation itself: what does he then but reveal himself to his servants, and as his manner is, first to his Englishmen"?[3] As Milton's turn of phrase indicates, the Puritans believed that England was the nation chosen to advance the Reformation further; the Tractarians believed that England had been chosen to prevent it going too far and, indeed, in Tract 41, Newman calls for a "second Reformation," which would reverse the extremes to which the old one had been carried.

Whereas the Tractarians were accused of turning their back on the Protestant identity of the Anglican church, they claimed that it was the Anglican church of their day that had drifted away from its Catholic identity. As it existed early in the 1830s, it had become more Protestant than was intended even by the first reformers. The Tracts give examples of disused rubrics and observances in the Book of Common Prayer itself that would in their day be condemned as "popish." In Tract 38, Newman complains that "Men seem to think that we are plainly and indisputably proved to be popish, if we are proved to differ from the generality of churchmen now-a-days. But what if it turn out that they are silently floating down the stream, and we are upon the shore?" Newman gives historical reasons for the drift towards Protestantism: the influence of the seventeenth-century Puritan movement, the rise of Methodism, political alliances with foreign Protestants, the latitudinarian or liberal school of the eighteenth century, led by Benjamin Hoadly. Pusey, viewing the English as a chosen people, naturally attributes its failings to the meddling of foreigners. When the solidly Catholic Book of Common Prayer of 1549 was issued, Pusey writes,

> The objections came entirely from without. When this, our genuine English liturgy, was framed, one foreign reformer only of any note (P. Martyr) had arrived in England; à Lasco, whose influence was subsequently most pernicious, and Bucer, came not until the liturgy was completed. But the kindness wherewith England has made itself the refuge of the oppressed, was in this case also abused. Immediately after the completion of the liturgy, we find the poor archbishop unhappily surrounded by foreigners, who had in their own countries rejected episcopacy, some, the doctrines of the sacraments also, and left their own countries because they went beyond the foreign reformation....
>
> The change in doctrine was now actually introduced, and recommended by the authority of Bishop Hooper, who had unhappily, during Henry VIII's reign, taken refuge in Zurich, and become acquainted with Bullinger, a friend of Zwingli.[4]

It is in the face of these historical misfortunes that Newman proposes his "second Reformation," which would "add [to the Thirty-Nine Articles] protests against the erastianism and latitudinarianism which have incrusted them" and "append to the Catechism a section on the power of the church." Or, again, "were an article framed (to speak by way of illustration) declaratory of the sanctity of places set apart to the worship of God and the reception of the saints that sleep, doubtless churchmen would be saved from many profane feelings and practices of the day" (Tract 41). Such measures would help reverse the Protestant drift of the Anglican church, and they would be true to the historical spirit of the church: "the English church, as such, is *not* Protestant, only politically, that is, externally, or so far as it has been made an establishment, and subjected to national and foreign influences. It claims to be merely *Reformed*, not Protestant." Evidence for this is "the emphatic omission of the word Protestant in all our services, even in that for the fifth of November" (Tract 71).[5]

A stumbling block to this view of the Anglican church, often brought forward by opponents of the Tractarians, is the Thirty-Nine Articles.[6] On the face of it the Articles are a thoroughly Protestant document, but most authorities agree that closer examination reveals something less obdurate. According to one modern source, "Though not ostensibly vague, they avoid unduly narrow definition. Much variety of interpretation has been put upon many of them without improperly straining the text, and probably this licence was deliberately intended by their framers."[7]

The Tractarians arrived at a similar understanding in a number of discussions, most of them by Newman. Newman argues over and over again that "Our Articles are not a body of divinity, but in great measure only protest against certain errors of a certain period of the church" (Tract 38).[8] In Tract 82, Newman offers a more fully worked out summary:

> I consider that the first five Articles have one definite, positive, dogmatic view, even that which has been, from the beginning, the Catholic and apostolic truth on which the church is built.
>
> From the Sixth to the Eighteenth, I conceive to have one certain view also, brought out in that particular form at the Reformation...
>
> In the remaining Articles, taken as a body, I think there is less strictness, perspicuity, and completeness of meaning. Some, though clear and definite in their meaning, are but negative, or protestant, as being directed against the Romanists; others, which are positive, are derived from various schools; in others the view is left open, or inchoate.

In Tract 90, Newman develops the implications of his earlier analyses in a detailed exposition of the Articles, designed "to show that... our articles..., the offspring of an uncatholic age, are, through God's good providence, to say the least, not uncatholic, and may be subscribed by those who aim at being catholic in heart and doctrine." Newman's Catholic interpretation of the Articles is carried out in this Tract, with all his skills in litigious argument on full display. An example is his treatment of Article XI, "Of the Justification of Man," which states that "We are accounted righteous before God, only for the merit of our Lord and Saviour Jesus Christ by faith, and not for our own works or deservings. Wherefore that we are justified by faith only is a most wholesome doctrine." Newman first points out that Catholic teaching makes baptism also a means or instrument of justification, so this doctrine must be accommodated by the Article:

> When, then, faith is called the sole instrument, this means the sole internal instrument, not the sole instrument of any kind. There is nothing inconsistent, then, in faith being the sole instrument of justification, and yet baptism also the sole instrument, and that at the same time, because in distinct senses; an inward instrument in no way interfering with an outward instrument. Baptism may be the hand of the giver, and faith the hand of the receiver.

Next, Newman argues that works too justify, but in another way again:

> Faith only may justify in one sense—good works in another:—and this is all that is here maintained. After all does not Christ only justify? How is it that the doctrine of faith justifying does not interfere with our Lord's being the sole justifier? . . . As, then, Christ justifies *in the sense* in which he justifies alone, yet faith also justifies in its own sense; so works, whether moral or ritual, may justify us in their own respective senses, though in the sense in which faith justifies, it only justifies.

This is far from Newman's most convincing writing. Such arguments needed to be made more fully and patiently. Instead, Newman's brisk convolutions outraged common-sense opinion no less than Protestant dogma. The storm over Tract 90 caused the Bishop of Oxford to request the termination of the Tracts. Newman was condemned by several bishops and censured in a statement issued by the heads of most of the Oxford colleges. All this led to Newman's withdrawal from an active role in the University and in the Tractarian movement.

Newman was on firmer ground when he argued that the basis for Catholic Anglicanism was the doctrine implicit in the liturgy, and that "the liturgy, as coming down from the apostles, is the depository of their complete teaching; while the Articles are polemical." This is a restatement of the ancient formula, *lex orandi lex credendi*, the law of prayer is the law of belief. That formula refers to the fact that, in the early church, liturgical tradition antedated any official creed and any agreement on what books made up the Bible. How the church prayed was the first guide to what it believed. This is true of Anglicanism also; the beliefs of the Anglican church have their most complete and authoritative statement in the Book of Common Prayer, where Catholic elements are much more evident than in the Thirty-Nine Articles.

In mapping their *via media*, the Tracts are very clear about their objections to the Protestant path, but their attitudes to the Roman path are more mixed and variable. Especially in the earlier Tracts, there is a good deal of reflex anti-papalism, in accord with the tradition that bundled together the persecutions of Queen Mary I, the treason of the Gunpowder Plot, and the absolutism of the Roman Catholic convert, King James II. The depth of this hostility is difficult to reimagine today (unless we compare it with the hostility in some parts of our society to Islam). In Tract 20, Newman is emphatic that "alas, AN UNION IS IMPOSSIBLE. Their communion is infected with heresy; we are bound to flee it, as a pestilence."[9] As late as Tract 79, he is serenely certain that "we are in no danger of becoming Romanists." In Tract 71, the first in a series "Against Romanism," Newman works his way through a full catalogue of the errors of Rome: the doctrine of transubstantiation, the distribution of communion in one kind only, compulsory confession, the doctrine of purgatory, the use of indulgences, the cult of images and saints, the claim of papal infallibility. Tract 79, the third of this series, takes up in great detail the doctrine of purgatory as an example of Rome's departure from Catholic teaching as defined by Vincent de Lérins.

Despite these faults of the Roman church, it is nevertheless true for the Tractarians that it has much to teach the Anglican church of the nineteenth century. In Tract 20, where he calls the Roman church a pestilence, Newman admits in almost the same breath that

> the papists have retained [the marks of a visible church]; and so they have the advantage of possessing an instrument, which is, in the first place, suited to the needs of human nature; and next, is a special gift of Christ, and so has a blessing with it. Accordingly we see that in its measure success follows their zealous use of it. They act with great force upon the imaginations of men. The vaunted antiquity, the universality, the unanimity of their church puts them above the varying fashions of the world, and the religious novelties of the day.

A similarly regretful sense of what the Roman church could offer, and what was lost in rejecting it, appears in Tract 34, "Rites and Customs of the Church," where Newman writes

> although . . . corrupt additions were made in the middle ages, yet . . . , as a whole, the Catholic ritual was a precious possession; and if we, who have escaped from popery, have lost not only the possession, but the sense of its value, it is a serious question whether we are not like men who recover from some grievous illness with the loss or injury of their sight or hearing;—whether we are not like the Jews returned from captivity, who could never find the rod of Aaron or the ark of the covenant.

This respectfulness is followed through in Newman's later treatment of the Roman breviary (Tract 75), which shows a willingness to participate more fully in Roman forms of devotion, and in which the Roman church appears less as a perversion of Catholicism than as a repository of true Catholicism, parts of which have been lost by the English church.

The idea that the Reformation entailed losses along with its necessary gains, the poignant thought that we have recovered from an illness but suffer the side-effects of the cure, is carried through in other Tracts, which depict an English church cut off from its full Catholic origins, incomplete, orphaned, exiled. Pusey writes an emotive elegy for what has been lost:

> It makes, in truth, a man's "eyes gush out with water," to see . . . how the glory of our church, the days of her youth, and her first love are departed: and to think what she might have been, had she stood in the old paths. "The virgin daughter of my people is broken with a great breach, with a very grievous blow."

Pusey here quotes Jeremiah's prophecy of the captivity of Judah (Jeremiah 14:17). This passage occurs in Tract 81, in which Pusey draws his comparison between the English nation and the people of Israel, both chosen by God: the English church resembles the people of Israel also in failing to live up to its high calling, and in therefore descending into captivity and exile.

For Isaac Williams in Tract 86, the whole history of the Anglican church, not just its recent history, is marked by its separation from the wider Catholic church and by its loss of the full tradition of Catholic worship. Williams sees the work of divine providence in the continuity of the liturgy from the early church to the English church, but he also sees the continuity as minimal, with many things lost. He notes in the Book of Common Prayer the disappearance of the word "altar," the shrinking of the daily offices from seven to two, the omission of anointing, the small place given to music. In a searching examination of the text of the Prayer Book, Williams observes how, in comparison with its medieval models, "entire Collects, or expressions in them, which imply the privileges of the faithful, or spiritual rejoicing, as of sons, are dropped; and prayers substituted in a lower tone." Hence, in the Collect for Advent Sunday,

> we find that in the ancient form there are the words "*who rejoice according to the flesh for the coming of thine only begotten Son.*" These are not in ours, but we have instead the sentence "*in the time of this mortal life in which thy Son Jesus Christ came to visit us in great humility.*"

For the Sunday after Ascension Day, "the Collect in the Parisian Breviary alludes to the gifts poured on the apostles, as if still continued in the church. That selected for our use is, that we be not left '*comfortless*,' '*ne nos derelinquas orphanos*.'" The Collect for the First Sunday after Easter originally used the language of the Preface for Easter Day, which has the beginning, " 'But chiefly are we bound to praise thee for the glorious Resurrection of thy Son Jesus Christ,'—and the end 'who by his death hath destroyed death, and by his rising to life again hath restored to us everlasting life.'" This form, "consisting entirely of thanksgiving," was replaced in the revision of 1662 by the original collect for Easter Tuesday, instead "containing the supplication, 'That we may so put away the leaven of malice and wickedness, that we may serve thee in pureness of living and truth.'"

The tendency of the Prayer Book is thus to set aside rejoicing and to emphasize repentance, to speak of Christians less as God's children than as God's servants, "to bring out, as it were by accident, the more humble and practical character" of Christianity. This, Williams argues, is not just a matter of national character, nor just a sign of Puritan influence. Beyond both of these things, it is a sign of how God wants us to regard ourselves in the aftermath of the Reformation. If we are viewed less as sons than as servants,

> it may be said that this term is more congenial to our language, or to the sober temper of our nation; but even were it so . . . there is a providential purpose to place us in this position. . . . from the instances already adduced in this treatise, it would seem that this "note of servile fear" is one peculiarly our own, as differing from the forms of prayer which we have in common with the Church of Rome.

The English church is in a condition of permanent repentance, not only for the past evils that the Reformation put to rights but also for the loss of the many valuable things that were sacrificed to the Reformation. The Anglican church appears in two guises in the Tracts for the Times: it is a precious gift, inherited from the early church, both catholic and reformed; it is also apt to fall away from this inheritance, not always able to "hold fast that which is good". This is a way of saying that the church is an institution both divine and human.

Endnotes

[1] Hostility towards Roman Catholicism, and especially to the papacy, remained at this time deeply rooted in the mentality of most Englishmen, and the Tractarians were no exception, as will appear more than once in this chapter. I regret any offence caused by their language. It was a period of unyielding religious controversy, and Roman Catholic authors expressed themselves in similarly vigorous terms. It must be remembered that the papacy was at this time not only a religious authority but also a secular power, ruling a considerable part of Italy, and that allegiance to the Pope could be regarded as incompatible with allegiance to the United Kingdom and its monarch. That was the view of *The Times* newspaper when Pope Pius IX reinstated Roman Catholic dioceses in England in 1850: it was

> a direct usurpation of a supreme spiritual power by a foreign priest over the length and breadth of this land, treating with equal arrogance the existence of our national church and the policy of our laws.... We can only receive it as an audacious and conspicuous display of pretensions to resume the absolute spiritual dominion of this island which Rome has never abandoned, but which, by the blessings of Providence and the will of the English people, she shall never accomplish.

[2] When Newman refers to "the faith which Ignatius, Cyprian, and Gregory received from the apostles," he is referring to the common faith that was maintained down to Nicaea in the eighth century, since Ignatius, Cyprian, and Gregory are bishops and saints of the first, third, and sixth centuries.

[3] *Areopagitica; a speech of Mr. John Milton for the liberty of unlicensed printing, to the Parliament of England* (1644), p. 31.

[4] This history is further canvassed in Tracts 38 and 72. Peter Martyr (Pietro Martire Vermigli), John à Lasco (or Laski), and Martin Bucer were continental Protestant leaders invited to England by Archbishop Cranmer, Vermigli and Bucer becoming professors of divinity at Oxford

and Cambridge. All three advised on revision of the Book of Common Prayer. Despite Pusey's account, there is no evidence that Cranmer was unhappy with their advice. Ulrich Zwingli and Heinrich Bullinger were leaders of Protestantism in Zurich.

5 After the Gunpowder Plot of 5 November 1606, a failed act of terrorism by Roman Catholics, a service of thanksgiving was added to the Book of Common Prayer. It was removed in 1859.

6 The "Articles of Religion," to give them their formal name, reached their final form in 1571. Until 1865 all clergy of the Church of England were required to subscribe to them, and until 1871 subscription to the Articles was required to matriculate at Oxford or to graduate from Cambridge. (After 1865, clergy were required to make the more limited acknowledgement that the Articles are "agreeable to the Word of God" and, since 1975, a still more limited acknowledgement has been required.)

7 *Oxford Dictionary of the Christian Church*, ed. F. L. Cross, 3rd edn revised, ed. E. A. Livingstone (Oxford: Oxford University Press, 2005), "Thirty-Nine Articles."

8 See also Tracts 71 (Newman) and 77 (Pusey).

9 The term, "heresy," in the first printing of Tract 20 (1833), was replaced by the milder "heterodoxy" in the second printing (1835), an early indication of the gradual change of view that would eventually see Newman join the Roman Catholic church.

The chapel of Keble College, Oxford. Such was the admiration for the work and life of John Keble that this college was founded in his memory at Oxford within four years of his death. The architecture of the college, by William Butterfield (1814-1900), is a high point in the Gothic Revival of the Victorian era, which coincided with the Oxford Movement. The two movements exercised a mutual influence on one another.

11

Tracts for the Times

Spiritual Life, or the Doctrines in Practice

The Tracts for the Times were initially provoked by a political crisis facing the Church of England in the 1830s, but that defence of the institutional church developed into a comprehensive theology of the church generally. A further aim that developed as the Tracts proceeded was to effect a new spiritualization of the church from within, a Catholic version of the Evangelical revival of the later eighteenth century. In part, this spirit, too, was created by the prospect of political persecution. Newman's apocalyptic vision of persecution in Tract 10 issues in a vision of a church renewed in its spiritual mission: "This may all come in our day; we must do our duty; go straight forward, looking neither to the right hand nor the left, 'in patience possessing our souls,' watching and praying, and so preparing for the evil day."

Other Tractarian writers also teach that the Christian life is a long path and a challenging discipline, never a simple matter of being born again and attaining unproblematic membership of the elect. In Tract 87, Isaac Williams warns that "all Divine and saving knowledge is derived by pains on the part of man, and requires preparation of the heart." He explains that

> every thing is difficult in proportion to its excellence and value. . . . For instance, if we take the subject of prayer, . . . how difficult is it to pray aright; so much so, that it were not too much to say, that it requires the very utmost stretch of our endeavours, the perfection of

our highest faculties, the labour of a long life, to learn to pray. The very best of men are but learners in this art, and become most sensible of their deficiencies.

To assist the student of this difficult art, meditations and prayers by Thomas Wilson (1663-1755), Bishop of Sodor and Man, are reprinted in a number of Tracts. Wilson's prayers are a reminder and an example of the duty of devotion, and they are a witness to the tradition of great teaching bishops in the Anglican church, one of the old treasures that the Tractarians hope to bring forth for their own times.

It goes without saying that the spirituality of the Tractarians is based in the Bible, and that they themselves are steeped in Biblical knowledge. The Tractarians cede nothing to their Evangelical brethren in marshalling Biblical materials. Detailed references to the history of Israel, to "preferring Abana and Pharpar to the waters of Jordan," to "Korah, Dathan, and Abiram, whose awful punishment you read of in the book of Numbers," spring readily to their memories. Newman instructs an imaginary correspondent in Tract 11 that, when seeking a theology of the church, "true doctrine and warm feelings are not enough. How am I to know what is enough? you ask. I reply, *by searching Scripture.*" This search demands the same seriousness and throws up no less challenges than the life of prayer: "no remarks, however just, can be much more than an assistance to you. You must search for yourself, and God must teach you." Keble's Tract 13 surveys the Old Testament lessons appointed for Sundays in the Book of Common Prayer, showing how the national history of Israel may be applied to the personal history of the individual Christian. Isaac Williams, in Tract 87, makes the same point about the Psalms: they are "full of divine meanings with respect to ourselves." In other words, the Tracts prompt us to find the spiritual meaning of the Old Testament narratives, translating their external battles and revenges into our own internal hatreds and treacheries. To cut down the enemies of Israel is to cut off our own personal errors or sins. To take possession of the Holy Land, to dwell in Jerusalem, is not about politics, ancient or modern, but about what it means to live in peace and harmony.

As well as their reliance on the Bible, the Tractarians also gave greatly increased prominence to the sacraments. The spiritual renewal encouraged by the Tracts included a renewed reverence for the Eucharist, with the revival of frequent communion, weekly or even daily—a practice almost unknown in the Anglican church of the time, and one that the Tractarians knew would be viewed with astonishment.[1] Tract 26 reprints parts of a sermon on "The necessity and advantage of frequent communion" by a divine of the late seventeenth century, William Beveridge, which contains sound advice for the spiritual life, written in a nimble prose that makes a welcome relief from the sometimes ponderous Victorian style of the Tractarians themselves:

> The oftener we do it, the more I expect we shall be at it, and the more benefit and comfort we shall receive from it. It is very difficult, if not impossible, for those who do it only now and then (as once or twice a year) ever to do it as they ought; for every time they come to it, they must begin as it were again; all the impressions which were made upon their minds at the last sacrament, being worn out before the next; and it being a thing they are not accustomed to, they are as much to seek how to do it now, as if they had never done it before. It is by frequent acts that habits are produced. It is by often eating and drinking this spiritual food that we learn how to do it, so as to digest and convert it into proper nourishment for our souls. And therefore I do not wonder that they who do it seldom, never do it as they ought, nor by consequence get any good by it; I should rather wonder if they did. But let any man do it often, and always according to the directions before laid down, and my life for his, he shall never lose his labour; but, whether he perceives it or not, he will grow in grace, and gather spiritual strength every time more and more.[2]

A similar concern with the detailed pattern of the spiritual life, including the effects of effort and habituation, occurs in Pusey's Tract 18, on fasting. There is a tendency today, even among Catholic Anglicans, to regard fasting as a merely negative exercise, insufficiently outward-looking, lacking generosity. Pusey's discussion threads together a sequence of ideas that invite us to reconsider the subject. He begins with the general value of fasting, which is directed not only towards resisting "temptations to luxury and self-indulgence" but also towards "spiritualizing of the affections." "Affections" in the language of the 1830s means something broader than it does today, not just fondness or tenderness but feelings and desires in general. To spiritualize feelings and desires sounds like an exercise in repression, an attempt to act against their natural character. But it may also be understood as a process that begins in awareness, in becoming conscious of feelings and desires rather than being driven by them unconsciously or half-consciously. One way of attaining this awareness is by not acting automatically at the prompting of every feeling or desire—in the first instance by fasting, but also by other kinds of discipline. Building on the awareness thus achieved, our feelings or desires may become the basis of self-knowledge and right action. This is to turn the "affections" to spiritual effect.

Pusey then addresses the value of having particular days laid down for fasting, as in the Book of Common Prayer. He sees the schedule of fasts as a preventative against spiritual laziness. To set aside days for fasting, and to observe them when they come around, whether or not we happen to be in the mood to do so, is to make sure that we carry through in practice something we know to be good in theory, and something enjoined by the Scriptures, as Pusey reminds us. In this connection, Pusey makes a psychological point about the benefits of simple regularity, which refers not to fasting only but to anything we practice on a regular basis, not making a great deal of it, just doing it:

> For let any one consider, from his childhood upwards, by what the greater part of his habits have been formed, and by what they are continued: not by any great acts or great sacrifices, . . . but by a succession of petty actions, whose effect he could not at any time foresee, or thought too minute to leave any trace behind them, and which have in fact, whether for good or for evil, made him what he is.

This understanding of the usefulness of simple regularity is similar to Beveridge's point about regular communion, and may derive from it.[3]

Examining the assumption that fasting is a merely negative exercise, Pusey answers that the "acquisition of the habit of self-denial, although an important object, is by no means the sole end of fasting. The great purpose, in connexion with which it is chiefly mentioned in Holy Scripture, is prayer." This is Pusey's view of the positive benefit of fasting. Again, it is perhaps because fasting causes us to step back from our usual habits, to observe our usual impulses (or "affections") in the act of cutting them off, that Pusey associates it with prayer, in its capacity as the careful and detailed self-examination of our feelings and motives and actions.

The prayerful aspect of fasting is important in "the times" to which the Tracts for the Times were addressed. Already in the 1830s, in the earliest stages of industrialization, urbanization, and faster communications, people were becoming aware of a change in the pace of life, and this awareness had penetrated even the cloistered calm of Oxford. Pusey therefore identifies a double utility in fasting for the 1830s: "In the present day, the first paramount evil which destroys its tens of thousands, is probably self-indulgence; the second which hinders thousands in their progress heavenwards, is the being 'busy and careful about many things,' whether temporal or spiritual." To counter the second of these evils, fasting separates us from our usual habits and our everyday activities, setting up a reflective state of mind or awareness, or a prayerful state, or what Pusey calls "tranquil retiring meditation."

Finally, fasting opens out into care for others, what Pusey calls "a more self-denying extensive charity." (Pusey the classical scholar means us to be cognisant of the Latin root of "extensive," *reaching out* to others, *stretching out* oneself). In the act of doing without, we are sensitized to having and not having, and therefore to the vast disparities of material well-being in the world around us. To those who take pride in the improvements in well-being that were taking place in England in the 1830s, Pusey addresses a challenge that reverberates no less in our own society:

let them inquire a little further, not only what wants are relieved, but what remediable misery remains unabated; or let them but observe generally the glaring contrasts of extremest luxury and softness, and pinching want and penury; between their own ceiled houses, and the houses of God which lie waste; or let them only trace out one single item in the mass of human wretchedness, disease, insanity, religious ignorance.

At the heart of Tractarian spirituality is an embrace of mystery, and a concomitant antagonism to an excessive or misplaced confidence in reason. This makes for a different emphasis from the embrace of reason by Hooker, Taylor, and Law, though all those writers agree that there are realms of religious belief and experience beyond the reach of reason. Those realms are the main subject of the Tractarian writers. Newman sees rationalism as the besetting failing of Protestantism, because Protestantism encourages the Christian to derive everything from the Bible, according to his or her own level of understanding, instead of accepting with faith the teachings of the church. Those teachings cannot, Newman insists, be reduced to a neat system. In Tract 73, *On the Introduction of Rationalistic Principles into Religion*, Newman reviews two books of nineteenth-century Protestant theology that, in his view, err by over-systematizing, seeking to enclose God's will and actions within the boundaries of human comprehension. These books thus become an occasion for a critique of rationalism in religion.[4]

Newman's review is long and repetitive, and few would now agree with all of it. Its central point is powerful, however. The two books seek to show how Christ's atonement conforms with God's justice. Newman denies that we have the capacity to propose such a thing as a theory of God's justice, because such a theory must reduce God's infinite powers and mysterious nature to the limits of human reason: "the dispensation thus being hewn and chiselled into an intelligible human system is represented, when thus mutilated, as affording a remarkable evidence of the truth of the Bible, an evidence level to the reason, and superseding the testimony of the apostles." If we cannot know God's will or truly fathom his work of salvation, why then do we call the Bible God's revelation? Newman's answer is that even revelation is still a mystery:

> It may seem a contradiction in terms to call Revelation a mystery; but is not the book of the Revelation of St. John as great a mystery from beginning to end as the most abstruse doctrine the mind ever imagined? yet it is even called a revelation. How is this? The answer is simple. No revelation [of God] can be complete and systematic, from the weakness of the human intellect; . . . When something is revealed—and only something, for all cannot be—there are forthwith difficulties and perplexities. A revelation is religious doctrine viewed on its illuminated side; a mystery is the self-same doctrine viewed on the side unilluminated. Thus religious truth is neither light nor darkness, but both together; it is like the dim view of a country seen in the twilight, with forms half extricated from the darkness, with broken lines, and isolated masses. Revelation, in this way of considering it, is not a revealed system [with the emphasis on *system*].

If Newman can himself seem too reliant on the devices of rationality, this passage shows that he has more than one side, that he communicates through both the bright illumination of reason and the poetic shadows appropriate to mystery.

Newman's most telling point against a theology that purports to understand a divine plan is that any such divine plan can really be no more than a projection of the personal wishes or hopes of the human mind that claims to encompass it. This criticism applies no less to the brisk equations of much Evangelical theology than to the more liberal theology at which Newman is taking aim in Tract 73. By what is on the face of it a paradox, rationality is the expression of emotional preferences. In the religious realm at any rate, the rational cannot function, because by definition God's mind and will are beyond human comprehension; we must accept mystery.

A second and more remarkable treatment of this subject, the necessary incompleteness of human religious understanding, is Isaac Williams's double Tract, *On Reserve in Communicating Reli-*

gious Knowledge (Tracts 80 & 87). If Williams's key term is "reserve," the term "mystery" better communicates the scope of his discussion.[5] Williams begins with the proposition that, in his earthly life, Christ revealed himself less fully than he might have done: he lived a mostly obscure life in the obscure province of Galilee; when he performed miracles he often demanded secrecy; he taught through parables, which are full of enigmas. All this, suggests Williams, is a sign that for us, too, there is a mystery about the nature of Christ and our relation to him, so that our understanding and our relationship unfold slowly. This process is witnessed in our gradually deepening understanding of the Lord's Prayer or the Ten Commandments, for example. But our understanding of the teachings is directly related to our conduct; again, reason will not achieve it. The only way to knowledge or understanding of "great truths," doctrines such as the Real Presence or free will, is through "practical obedience"; we can truly understand the Beatitudes only by acting them out:

> All these topics contain great sacred truths of the very highest possible importance that we should know; but if we attempt to arrive at any knowledge of them by speculation, or any other mode but that of practical obedience, that knowledge is withheld . . . in the same manner that it was of the highest importance that they should know our Lord; but unless they were sincerely and humbly seeking him, he was hid from them.

It follows that, both in his lifetime and in ours, Christ was and must be known by different people in different ways, and no one can be sure that theirs is the one true way:

> as the Gospels indicate . . . that the benefit conferred on every individual was exactly according to his faith, to the effort he made to ask, or to touch the hem of our Saviour's garment, so do the Fathers also teach that exactly according to the advancement of holiness of life, or the effort to advance, does Christ disclose the eternal Father.

Or, to express it more simply: " 'they shall see God,'—see Him according to each of his various attributes, which their own characters most open to them." Williams points out that the church does, or should, offer different pathways:

> She contains as it were within herself numerous channels or modes of access. . . . Her sacramental ordinances are, in fact, ways to that invisible Jerusalem, that celestial fellowship, and the city of the living God. The progressive states of proficiency in the school of Christ have been termed the *via purgativa*, or the way of repentance; the *via illuminativa*, or the way of Christian knowledge; and the *via unitiva*, or the way of charity and union with God. . . . Church principles contain within them these modes of bringing men to the knowledge of, and to union with God, who dwelleth in secret.

The Tracts can be rigid in their insistence on every last jot and tittle of orthodox doctrine, so it is gratifying to meet this recognition of different understandings of God, which has another mark of the catholic—inclusiveness.

It is in the context of his defence of "reserve," or mystery, that Williams introduces his criticism, discussed above, of the Evangelical practice of "bringing forward the Atonement *explicitly* and *prominently* on all occasions." When St Paul brings forward the doctrine to the Romans and Galatians, argues Williams, it is only because discussion of the doctrine was current at those places. In general, however, "The singular characteristic of St. Paul, as shown in all his epistles and speeches, seems to have been a going out of himself to enter into the feelings and put himself in the circumstances of others." In St Paul, then, there is a broad human sympathy, a recognition of the variety of human experience, not a rigid doctrine of the atonement. The true way to preach Christ crucified is

> the necessity of our being crucified to the world, it is our humiliation together with him, mortification of the flesh, being made conformable to his sufferings and his death. It was a doctrine which was "foolishness to the wise and an offence to the Jew," on account of the abasement of the natural man which it implied. Whereas, the notion now

prevailing is attractive to the world, in the naked way in which it is put forth, so as rather to diminish, than increase, a sense of responsibility and consequent humiliation.

Like all aspects of Christianity, Christ crucified is understood and preached through the experience of living out the faith, not by a system of ideas. Such insights into the religious life, prayer, and morality, clearly based on a conscientious attempt to live out the teachings that they proclaimed, contributed greatly to the influence of the Tractarians. The Tracts for the Times are concerned with doctrine *and* action, faith *and* works, the visible church as the body of all Christians *and* the inner life of the individual Christian who is a member of that body.

Endnotes

[1] Jeremy Taylor was an earlier voice advocating more frequent communion: see pp. 83-4.

[2] More of Beveridge's discussion of communion appears in Tract 81, and frequent communion is urged also in Tracts 6, 18, and 73.

[3] Pusey's Tract 18 appeared eight weeks before Tract 26, but it is possible that he would have known about its contents, and even possible that he recommended its publication. Pusey quotes a thought along similar lines by Johann Wolfgang Goethe: " 'Neither in moral or religious, more than in physical and civil matters,' says a very acute observer of human nature, 'do people willingly do any thing suddenly or upon the instant; they need a succession of the like actions, whereby a habit may be formed; the things which they are to love, or to perform, they cannot conceive as insulated and detached.'" This is a rare appearance in the Tracts by a near-contemporary continental writer.

[4] The books, once widely read but now forgotten, are: Thomas Erskine, *Remarks on the Internal Evidence for the Truth of Revealed Religion* (Edinburgh, 1820; 9th edition 1829); and Jacob Abbott, *The Corner-Stone, or, a familiar illustration of the principles of Christian truth* (Boston and New York, 1834; two London editions, 1834; another, 1835). Tract 73 was published in 1836 and must therefore have been prompted by Abbott's book, which linked itself in Newman's mind with Erskine's earlier one.

[5] The term, "reserve", was suggested by Newman (*Oxford Dictionary of National Biography*, "Isaac Williams").

Illustration Credits

p. 11, Huntington Library, San Marino, California.

p. 20, Huntington Library, San Marino, California.

p. 33, Huntington Library, San Marino, California.

p. 40, Photograph by Chris Beckett, licence https://creativecommons.org/licenses/by-nc-nd/2.0/.

p. 58, (Above) Photograph by Nick MacNeill, licence https://creativecommons.org/licenses/ccby- sa/2.0.

(Below) The Miriam and Ira D. Wallach Division of Art, Prints and Photographs: Print Collection, The New York Public Library. The New York Public Library Digital Collections. 1690. http://digitalcollections.nypl.org/items/8c13a117-d23b-3f6f-e040-e00a18063cf058.

p. 76, Photograph by Derek Harper, licence https://creativecommons.org/licenses/cc by-sa/2.0/.

p. 95, Licence https://commons.wikimedia.org/wiki/File:Lime_Grove_Putney_(1846)_home_of_the_Gibbon_family_where_William_Law_walked_with_John_Byrom.jpg.

p. 113, Photograph by Development and Alumni Engagement Office, Oriel College, Oxford.

p. 122, From William Francis Barry, *Newman* (London: Hodder & Stoughton, 1904).

p. 141, Photograph by the author.

p. 154, Photograph by the author.

Index

Aaron 66-8
Addison, Joseph 103
Agnus Dei 12
à Lasco, John 145, 152n
Andrewes, Bishop Lancelot 14, 27
Apocrypha 22
Apology of the Church of England 32, 39, 41
Aquinas, St Thomas 9, 42, 48
Aramaic 22, 23
Augustine, St 34, 36, 48

Bacon, Anne, Lady 34
Bancroft, Archbishop Richard 27-9, 32
Bernard of Clairvaux, St 37
Beveridge, Bishop William 157, 159, 164n
Bishops' Bible 26-7
Böhme, Jakob 109n
Bonaventura, St 81
Book of Common Prayer viii-ix, 9-19, 34, 36, 72, 78. 84, 112, 121n, 144-5, 148, 150, 156, 158
Bowden, J. W. 129, 140
Brett, Bishop Thomas 142
Brown, David vii
Bucer, Martin 12, 145, 152-3n
Buddha (Siddartha Gautama) 110n
Bullinger, Heinrich 145, 153n
Byrd, William 13

Calvin, John 9, 13-14, 25-6, 42, 47-8, 51, 54, 60, 101, 129

Cambridge (city and university) 27, 57, 59-60, 70, 77, 93, 153n
Castle of Perseverance 75n
Charles I 15, 26, 77, 87, 136n
Charles II 15
Christian Year (Keble) 111-6
Coleridge, Samuel Taylor 84
Cosin, Bishop John 14
Country Parson (Herbert) 57, 59, 62, 65, 68-75
Coverdale, Miles 24-5
Cranmer, Archbishop Thomas 12, 16-18, 153n
Cromwell, Oliver 78
Cyprian, St 34, 39, 140, 152n

Directory for the Public Worship of God 14
Donne, John 85
Dryden, John 103

Ecclesiastical Polity (*Of the Laws of Ecclesiastical Polity: Eight Books*) (Hooker) 41
Eden, C. P. 130-1, 133, 139
Edward VI 10, 25
Elizabeth I 13, 15, 31, 79, 90n
Epictetus 87
Erasmus, Desiderius 48
Estienne, Robert 25
Eusebius 35, 94

Faerie Queen (Spenser) 75n
Francis de Sales, St 88

Gardiner, Bishop Stephen 12
Geneva Bible 25-9
Great Bible 25
Great Exemplar (Taylor) 81-4
Gregorian Calendar 15
Gunpowder Plot 15, 148, 153n

Hammond, Henry 136n
Harrison, Benjamin 129, 131
Henry VIII 10, 13, 16, 25, 28, 91n, 145
Herbert, George viii, 57-79, 85, 93, 107-8, 109n, 111, 120
Hoadly, Bishop Benjamin 96, 98, 109n, 126, 144
Holy Dying (Taylor) 88-90
Holy Living (Taylor) 84-8
Hooker, Richard viii, 31, 35, 40-56, 78, 81, 87, 100, 124, 130, 137n, 144, 160
Hooper, Bishop John 145
Howley, Archbishop William 126

Ignatius Loyola, St 81, 85

James I 13, 26, 59
James II 93, 148
Jewel, Bishop John 31-9, 41-2, 52, 56, 59, 124, 142
Johnson, Samuel 84, 103

Keble, John 7, 90n, 96, 111-21, 123, 125, 127-8, 138n, 156
Ken, Bishop Thomas 136n
King James Bible viii, 16, 21-30

Latin Mass 10
Laud, Archbishop William 14-15, 63, 74, 77-8, 87, 105
Law, William 60, 69, 74, 93-110, 120
Liberty of Prophesying (Taylor) 79-81
Litany 9, 14
Locke, John 90n, 102
Ludolf of Saxony 81
Luther, Martin 23-5, 48

Magnificat 10
Manning, Henry Cardinal 133, 138n, 142
Marriott, Charles 133, 142
Mary I 12, 13, 24, 25, 31, 32, 93, 148
Matthew's Bible 24-5
Milton, John 90n, 144, 152n
Morley, William 13

Newman, John Henry Cardinal 1, 96, 117, 123-53
Newton, Isaac 102
Nicene Creed 117

Osborne, John 84
Overall, Bishop John 27
Oxford (city and university) ix, 23, 25, 27, 41, 111-2, 123-5, 138n, 139, 148, 153n, 159
Oxford Movement (see also Tractarians) 56, 82, 94, 97, 109n, 111-2, 116-7, 119, 121n, 123, 137n

Palmer, William 129, 139
Parable of the Talents 103

Paul, St 37, 79, 83, 84, 91, 118, 163

Pearson, Bishop John (*Exposition of the Creed*) 128

Perceval, A. P. 126

Phillpotts, Bishop Henry 124

Pius V 80

Plato 50, 73, 87

Plutarch (*Tranquility of the Soul*) 87

Pope, Alexander 103, 105

printers 25

Prudentius 75n

Pusey, Edward Bouverie 124-6, 134, 137n, 143-5, 150, 153n, 157-60, 164n

Quiñones, Cardinal Francisco de 12

Rheims-Douai Bible 26

Rogers, John 24

Rossetti, Christina 7

Sarum Missal 17

Septuagint 22

Serious Call to a Devout and Holy Life (Law) 93, 95-109

Sheldon, Archbishop Gilbert 15

Song of Solomon 30n

Sydney, Anglican Diocese of 3

Tallis, Thomas 13

Taylor, Jeremy viii, 60, 69, 77-91, 93, 100, 160, 164n

Te Deum 10

Tertullian 35, 48

Theophrastus 103

Thirty-Nine Articles ix, 15, 21-2, 36, 123, 140, 144, 146, 148

Tractarians (see also Oxford Movement) 5-6, 69, 123-7, 130-3, 139-40, 142-4, 146, 149, 152n, 156-7, 164

Tracts for the Times ix, 18n, 90n, 111, 123-64

Trent, Council of 26, 32, 34, 38-9

Tye, Christopher 13

Tyndale, William 23-5, 28-9

Uzzah 66

Vaughan, Henry 85

Vermigli, Peter Martyr 12, 152-3n

Vincent of Lérins, St 37, 142-3, 148

Voltaire 102

Vulgate Bible 23, 26

Webster, John (*Duchess of Malfi*) 91n

Wesley, John 84, 96

Whittingham, William 25

Wied, Archbishop Hermann von 12, 17

Williams, Isaac 18n, 130, 135-6, 150-1, 155-6, 161-3, 164n

Williams, Archbishop Rowan vii

Wilson, Bishop Thomas 156

Wren, Bishop Matthew 14

Wycliffe, John 23

Zwingli, Ulrich 153

Anthony Miller was formerly Associate Professor and Chair of the Department of English at the University of Sydney. He holds degrees from the Universities of Western Australia, Cambridge, and Harvard, and held visiting appointments at the University of Minnesota and St John's College, Oxford. His books include studies of *Roman Triumphs and Early Modern English Culture* and of Shakespeare's *Antony and Cleopatra*, and editions of Shakespeare's *Richard III* and *Julius Caesar*. Much of the content of this book was originally delivered as addresses at the Anglican Parish of Christ Church St Laurence, Sydney, where he was a Warden 2013-22.

www.ingramcontent.com/pod-product-compliance
Lightning Source LLC
Chambersburg PA
CBHW052048300426
44117CB00012B/2020